Advance Praise for **Tantric Sex f** P9-DUH-576

❖   ❖   ❖

"I have spent most of my career studying women's sexual heath in laboratory settings and know nothing about Tantra. I found this book to be informative and intriguing. *Tantric Sex for Busy Couples* is a well-written basic guide for those who want to learn more and incorporate Tantra into their lives."

— Beverly Whipple, PhD, author of *The G-Spot &
Other Discoveries About Human Sexuality*
and *The Science of Orgasm*

"As a lifelong advocate of how body awareness can bring us into con-nection with the present moment, I was delighted to encounter this book. With charming anecdotes and refreshing clarity, the Daffners offer a practical guide to that most elusive of states: true intimacy. Highly recommended!"

— Ann Weiser Cornell, PhD,
author of *The Power of Focusing*
and *The Radical Acceptance of Everything*

"Greater sexual freedom has not created more sexually satisfied people. In fact, sex for many people only deepens their feelings of emptiness, aloneness, and sadness. This book opens the way for sex being an integral part of fulfilling our basic need for an emotionally meaningful connection."

— Jordan Paul, PhD, author of *Becoming Your Own Hero*
and coauthor of *Do I Have to Give Up Me to Be Loved by You?*

"Richard and Diana's book *Tantric Sex for Busy Couples* is a helpful tool in keeping busy couples juicy and romantically connected."

— Charles Muir, author of *Tantra: the Art of Conscious Loving*
and *Awakening the Goddess and Freeing the Female Orgasm*

"It is unusual for an author to approach intimate sexuality in a manner that is easy and comfortable to her readers. In this wonderful book, Diana Daffner does just that. Physical love may be expressed in many different ways. The path shown in *Tantric Sex for Busy Couples* is accessible for modern lovers."

— Felice Dunas, PhD, author of *Passion Play: Ancient Secrets for a Lifetime of Health and Happiness Through Sensational Sex*

"Diana and Richard's book is a creative blend of the practices of Tai Chi and Tantra sex. The book, *Tantric Sex for Busy Couples*, takes the reader through a series of woven practices with the personal perspectives and experience of Diana and her husband, Richard. Their book is reader friendly, instructional, and delightfully candid."

— Sally Valentine, PhD, AASECT certified sex therapist and Tantra facilitator

"This is one of the most practical, easy-to-understand, and playful books I have seen on the Tantric path to intimacy. Free of the usual Eastern jargon that so many others try to impress their readers with, Diana (and her sidebar husband/lover, Richard) go deep lightly. You'll actually be able to use this book from the start to make your life and most intimate relationships more joyfully fulfilling."

— Robert Sachs, author of *The Passionate Buddha: Wisdom on Intimacy and Enduring Love*

"The Daffners' simple intimacy ceremonies speak directly to the only part of the human brain that can fall in love—or *stay* in love. This primitive part of the brain finds touch, eye contact, and attentiveness far more persuasive than discussion, or even self-centered passion. Both men and women will be amazed at their effectiveness."

— Marnia Robinson, author of *Cupid's Poisoned Arrow: From Habit to Harmony in Sexual Relationships*

"Diana tells her story with grace, humor, and wisdom. She gives us hope that our own intimate relationships can shine as brightly, and provides tools to help us get there. Her unique perspective, and Richard's comments, will inspire and encourage couples to learn even more about Tantra."

— Drs. Bryan and Light Miller,
authors of *Ayurveda and Aromatherapy*
and *Ayurvedic Remedies for the Whole Family*

"*Tantric Sex for Busy Couples: How to Deepen Your Passion in Just Ten Minutes a Day* is a highly readable book, providing practical inspiration for deepening into heart-centered presence. Diana and Richard speak honestly, eloquently, and from their personal experience in the Art of Love."

— Elysabeth Williamson, author of *The Pleasures
and Principles of Partner Yoga*

"Sex is important nourishment for a marriage. This book provides worthwhile suggestions for accomplishing real intimacy with your partner."

— Michele Weiner-Davis,
best-selling author of *The Sex Starved Marriage*.
www.DivorceBusting.com

"The Daffners have found a very natural way to have great sex, and they share it with us from their hearts. Having attended their classes, and now reading the book, I especially recognize and applaud the power of their 'Peaceful Passion' approach. It has helped bring my own relationship to a higher level."

— Dr. Howard Peiper, ND, nominated for a Pulitzer Prize,
best-selling author of *The A.D.D. & A.D.H.D. Diet*
and *Natural Solutions for Sexual Enhancement*.

Other titles in the Positively Sexual series

❊   ❊   ❊

Ordering

Trade bookstores in the U.S. and Canada please contact:

Publishers Group West
1700 Fourth Street, Berkeley CA 94710
Phone: (800) 788-3123   Fax: (800) 351-5073

Hunter House books are available at bulk discounts for textbook course
adoptions; to qualifying community, health-care, and government organizations;
and for special promotions and fund-raising. For details please contact:

Special Sales Department
Hunter House Inc., PO Box 2914, Alameda CA 94501-0914
Phone: (510) 865-5282   Fax: (510) 865-4295
E-mail: ordering@hunterhouse.com

Individuals can order our books from most bookstores,
by calling **(800) 266-5592**, or from our website at
www.hunterhouse.com

tantric sex

for busy

couples

How to Deepen Your Passion
in Just Ten Minutes a Day

❖　❖　❖

Diana Daffner, M.A.

with Richard Daffner

Hunter House PUBLISHERS

Keep Love Alive!
♡ Diana
& Richard

Hunter House Inc., Publishers
PO Box 2914
Alameda CA 94501-0914

Library of Congress Cataloging-in-Publication Data

Daffner, Diana.
Tantric sex for busy couples : how to deepen your passion in just ten
minutes a day / Diana Daffner, with Richard Daffner. — 1st ed.
p. cm. — (Positively sexual)
Includes index.
ISBN 978-0-89793-515-9 (pbk.)
1. Sex instruction. 2. Tantrism. 3. Sex customs—India.
I. Daffner, Richard. II. Title.
HQ64.D34 2009
613.9'6—dc22   2008054203

Project Credits

Cover Design: Brian Dittmar Graphic Design

Illustrator: Kaylene Simmons Rudd	Senior Marketing Associate: Reina Santana
Book Production: John McKercher	Publicity Associate: Sean Harvey
Copy Editor: Mary Miller	Rights Coordinator: Candace Groskreutz
Customer Service Manager: Christina Sverdrup	
Proofreader: John David Marion	Order Fulfillment: Washul Lakdhon
Indexer: Diana Daffner	Administrator: Theresa Nelson
Editor: Alexandra Mummery	Computer Support: Peter Eichelberger
Publisher: Kiran S. Rana	

Printed and Bound by Bang Printing, Brainerd, Minnesota

Manufactured in the United States of America

9 8 7 6 5 4 3 2 1   First Edition   09 10 11 12 13

Contents

❄   ❄   ❄

Important Note

The material in this book is intended to provide a review of information regarding Tantra Tai Chi. Every effort has been made to provide accurate and dependable information. We believe that the sensuality advice given in this book poses no risk to any healthy person. However, if you have any sexually transmitted diseases, we recommend consulting your doctor before using this book.

Therefore, the publisher, authors, and editors, as well as the professionals quoted in the book, cannot be held responsible for any error, omission, professional disagreement, or dated material, and are not liable for any damage, injury, or other adverse outcome of applying any of the information resources in this book. If you have questions concerning the application of the information described in this book, consult a qualified professional.

We dedicate
this book to the
many couples who have
attended our Intimacy Retreats
and affirmed for us the value
of these teachings. Although
this book cannot convey the entire
Intimacy Retreat experience,
we hope that it will remind
and inspire you to keep
intimacy and love alive
in your relationships.

Diana & Richard
Daffner

Acknowledgments

❋   ❋   ❋

First of all, I would like to acknowledge my parents, whose love for each other provided my first working model of a relationship.

For the development of this mind/body approach to intimacy, I extend my gratitude to Robert Nadeau, my Aikido and meditation teacher, who taught me that energy is real and that when I connect with the source of energy within me, I can then connect more fully with my partner; to Justin Stone, who originated T'ai Chi Chih®, and gifted the world with an easy way to experience energy flow; to Chungliang Al Huang, who taught me that T'ai Chi is a continually evolving practice; and to Bhante Wimala, a Buddhist monk from Sri Lanka, who taught me that the heart is real and that when I connect with my heart, I can look at life with different eyes.

None of the above knew that I would take their teachings and transform them into a program of sexual intimacy. They might not even approve. But I acknowledge each for their contribution to the foundation of Tantra Tai Chi.

I would also like to acknowledge Zan Butterfly Deer Woman, who taught me the value and power of ceremony; Satya Winkleman, who first pointed out to me that T'ai Chi was indeed a form of ritual; Drs. Bryan and Light Miller, who walk their talk as Tantra teachers, Ayurvedic healers, and deeply committed practitioners of the art of conscious relationship; Cia Ricco, sex therapist, for offering gentle and helpful suggestions from her own experienced perspective; and Jim and Lynda Harden, whose loving and professional support has meant so much to me.

I also acknowledge the many other teachers, colleagues, and authors who have inspired me in person or through their writings in the field of sexuality, including, but not limited to, Margo Anand, Dr. Barnaby Barratt, Dr. Deepak Chopra, Suzie Heumann, Dr. Felice Dunas, Patricia Johnson and Mark Michaels, Dr. Victoria Lee, Al Link and Pala Copeland, Barry Long, Daniel Mars, Carolyn Muir, Charles Muir, Dr. Paul Pearsall, Diana Richardson, Osho/Bhagwan Rajneesh, Robert Sachs, Marnia Robinson, Dr. Howard Pieper, Dr. David Schnarch, Jeffery Tye, Joyce and Barry Vissell, Dr. Beverly Whipple, and Catherine Yronwode.

I thank all of my friends who have supported my writing intentions since day one. You know who you are and how important you are to me.

And most of all, I am grateful for the gift of a loving relationship that I enjoy with my husband, Richard. Our wedding vows were to "learn alongside one another what it means to be human, what it means to love another person for a whole lifetime." In this book, Richard has helped me share some of what we have learned so far.

Introduction

Tantric lovemaking is a sacred ceremony that creates a sense of intimacy and passion. The words may sound esoteric but the experiences are practical and down-to-earth. Based on principles of Eastern teachings, the concepts of awareness and presence transcend cultural boundaries. And contrary to popular thinking, it is possible to benefit from these teachings without engaging in lengthy sexual rituals.

This book is a personal story, our way of sharing with you what has worked for my husband, Richard, and me in our long-term relationship. More importantly, it is about what matters to us, a couple with all the usual challenges that come with being in a relationship. In our busy lives, we find ten minutes a day to embrace and honor the love that we share.

No belief system, no adherence to any spiritual path is needed to benefit from these teachings. And most surprisingly, no pumped-up sexual drive or potency is needed to enjoy tantric sex.

Tantric sex can transform your relationship into an affair of love, regardless of how long you have been together, how old you are, or whether you are heterosexual, bisexual, gay, or lesbian.

Because I am a woman married to a man, the language I use and the references I make are often heterosexually based. However, tantric loving is appropriate for all couples. And if you are currently between relationships, the exercises in this book provide hope and guidance for your future.

My story opens with a poem, "The Lover's Touch," which came to me one evening long ago. Later that night, I visited a friend in the hospital, a psychotherapist who could no longer speak and had entered her final days. I read her the poem. Letter by letter, she laboriously spelled out a reply to me on an alphabet board that she kept by her bed: "You must publish this." She wanted me to know that others would want to hear these words, that others would recognize within themselves the same yearning for intimacy.

I hope this book helps you and your partner find the intimate and sacred space within your own relationship.

When people participate in ceremony, they enter a sacred space. Everything outside of that space fades in importance, Time takes on a different dimension, Emotions flow more freely, And the bodies of participants become filled with the energy of life, And this energy reaches out and blesses the creation around them. All is made new, Everything becomes sacred.

SUN BEAR,
Native American
medicine teacher

RICHARD SAYS *I have had the privilege of being Diana's husband for over twenty years. From the day I met her, I knew she had a message to bring to the world. I knew that the love I felt in her presence was not just for me alone, and that I would have to share her gifts with others. This book is one of those gifts. What she describes here is true. Together we have found a way to let our sexual energy take us into a magical experience. You can too. Diana and I enjoy tantric sex every day and I can't imagine why anyone in a relationship wouldn't want to. It doesn't take very long. We ourselves have a ten-minute commitment that you'll read about it in this book. Go ahead and schedule appointments with your own partner. Let intimacy and love shape your day. You'll both be glad.*

The Lover's Touch

The Lover's Touch

The Lover asked:
How would you like me to touch you?

The Lover answered:
I would like you to touch me as if you were going away tomorrow,
far, far away, and you wanted to remember the feel of my body,
the texture of my skin, the hills and valleys that make up
the landscape of who I am.

I would like you to touch me as if you were blind, knowing that you
love me, but unable to see me. Touch my face, my breasts, my belly,
my toes…learn what I "look" like, imagine me in your mind
as your hands explore my shape.

I would like you to touch me as if your hands were healing hands,
radiating love energy with every stroke. Feel the energy penetrating
through skin, through flesh, entering into the cells of my body.

I would like you to touch me as if you gained your nourishment
through your hands. Feed on me, drink deeply,
and draw from your touch the love that I hold for you.

*I would like you to touch me as if you were feeding me
through your hands, as if by your touch I am nourished
and sustained. Every inch of me cries out for your touch,
yearns to be fed.*

*I would like you to touch me as if your hand were a feather,
lightly caressing the edge of my being.*

*I would like you to touch me as if your hands were paintbrushes,
and as you caress me, you are coloring me in brilliant,
sparkling, dazzling hues.*

*I would like you to touch me as if you were erasing the outer me,
allowing me to reveal my inner self to you.*

*I would like you to touch me as if you had carved a sculpture
and were now feeling its finish, smoothing out any rough areas,
enjoying the finished product.*

*I would like you to touch me as if your hands were fire,
burning away the dross and leaving only the pure gold of my soul.*

*I would like you to touch me as if your hands were sponges,
soaking up the essence of my being.*

*I would like you to caress me as if I were made of dry clay,
and by dampening my skin, you enliven my spirit.*

I would like you to touch me as if my skin were soft velvet.

*I would like you to touch me as if you were a musician,
and your touch brought forth different sounds
from different parts of me.*

*I would like you to touch me as if I were a rare jewel,
precious and valuable.*

I would like you to touch me as if I were your Lover.

When I wrote these words some years ago, I felt within me an incredible yearning for meaningful touch from my husband, Richard. It was a cry for intimate connection from the deepest level of my soul.

RICHARD SAYS   *I don't easily recognize this emotional longing in myself. Then again, I really don't identify emotions much at all. Diana's drive for connection has been a great motivator to take us to places I didn't even know existed. Now, I can't imagine sex without it.*

Today he and I engage in a way of making love that brings a delighted smile to every pore of both of our bodies. Beyond touch, beyond the physical caress, we now share a soulful blending, a feeling of love in our hearts that meets and exceeds the longing that this poem expresses.

You or your partner may also be yearning for more intimacy in your relationship. It may be about enjoying more or better sex, or developing deeper, more heartfelt feelings and communications. Being deliciously and profoundly connected with your significant other is one of the main attractions and delights of a relationship. I consider myself lucky to have an intimate partner, and, like you, I want our relationship to be the best it can be. I want to continue experiencing the love that brought us together. I want to remain in love, to fall in love, to be in love, every day. The honeymoon itself may be over, but love can—and must—

continue to be acknowledged and honored "as long as we both shall live."

Sure, it is great to have a partner to help pay the mortgage and assist with all the other chores and responsibilities of family and home life, but it is the shared moments of intimate connection that make a relationship really worthwhile. We all want more of those moments. That must be why, despite a high divorce rate, couples continue to choose the path of life partnership.

I don't know if being in a relationship—being committed to one significant other—is the best way to move through this mysterious dance of life. It is certainly not the only way. What I do know is that most of my single friends and clients seek a caring, intimate partner into whose arms they might joyously melt. This urge to merge seems to be a basic human desire. We long to be held, to be truly known, to be truly touched. And most importantly, we long to be known and cherished in this way by the "love of our life," our significant other. It is this merging, this knowing of one to the other, that indeed makes our love relationships significant.

The exercises and lovemaking practices presented in this book are a way of acknowledging that significance. As Richard and I have done, you and your partner can also learn to transform your relationship into a meaningful love affair, even if you can find only ten minutes a day.

Intimacy in New Relationships

In the beginning of a relationship, when love is new, there is a natural focus on making contact. Getting to know each other—physically, emotionally, and mentally—automatically turns our attention toward one another, while heightening and brightening the experience of sexual intimacy.

When we first met, Richard and I lived in different cities. We were together only every other weekend. Distance and anticipation, and maybe the lack of cell phones in those days, added spice to our inevitable bedroom ballet (which sometimes took place in the kitchen or on the living room floor). We were hungry to discover each other.

Later on, after the wedding and honeymoon period, our lovemaking succumbed to the clichés about married sex, becoming more routine and less satisfying. Something was definitely missing. The sexual activity continued, but it was not adding "significance" or meaning to our lives. Maybe daily availability was decreasing our appetite.

I was the first to notice it. Our loving had become more hurried, more monotonous—less about loving and more about sexual release, primarily for Richard.

In my quest to change the situation, I could have taken things into my own hands. I often did, but since I didn't usually share those times with Richard, it didn't improve things between us. I certainly could have been more direct with him as to what I needed for my specific sexual satisfaction. Although I had come of age in the "free love" era of the sixties, I still wasn't comfortable talking openly about my sexual desires. Had I done so, our sex life would most likely have improved. But I was really looking for something more than just a better sex life. I was longing for an intimately loving experience that would put a smile on my face and a glow in my heart.

What I did say to Richard was, "This isn't working for me. I know our lovemaking can be much greater for both of us. There's a whole other level of intimacy that is possible." I believed that our loving could be an opportunity to develop not only a connection with each other but also with our deepest source of being. I knew my body was the doorway to my soul, to a place within me where love reigns supreme, and I wanted to walk through that doorway with Richard.

> *I believe the greatest gift I can conceive of having from anyone is to be seen, heard, understood, and touched by them. The greatest gift I can give is to see, hear, understand, and touch another person. When this is done, I feel contact has been made.*
>
> VIRGINIA SATIR,
> originator of
> family therapy

His response was, "You're probably right, but you'll have to take us there." Although he was aware of the growing monotony of our sexual times together, he was nonetheless being adequately satisfied. Therefore, he wasn't particularly motivated to change. Fortunately, for both of us, and for the many couples who have since attended our Intimacy Retreat workshops, he recognized the potential in what I was asking for. He also knew that with my background as a teacher of energy awareness, massage, Aikido, and meditation, I would find a way to bring enlightenment into our bedroom.

RICHARD SAYS *Obviously, she did find a way. I wasn't the easiest of students. Sometimes the last person you want to listen to is your wife. However, the subject matter, sex, helped hold my normally short attention span. Diana had to learn how to express herself to me without pushing my male defensive buttons. More than once, I told her, "You're probably right, but your presentation sucks." Luckily, for both of us, she didn't give up.*

Our quest for deeper loving took us beyond the mechanics of better sex into the vastly more fulfilling world of soulful and sacred intimacy. We discovered how to create an incredible joining of our bodies, hearts, and souls. When we apply the powerful principles that you will learn about in this book, our focus during lovemaking is no longer on climax or "reaching" orgasm. Our daily ten-minute tantric sex practice is not even dependent on erections or sexual drive. Yet it provides us both with the sexual fulfillment of orgasmic energy and with the emotional fulfillment of keeping intimacy alive.

Intimacy Requires Attention

When the dating/mating rush of a new relationship dissipates, other activities seem to fill up more and more space in our lives until intimacy is no longer a central focus. Love may still be strong but the ongoing *experience* of love, the *feeling* that comes from recognizing and acknowledging that deep connection, often begins to evaporate.

Keeping intimacy alive requires the same kind of interested attention we gave each other in the beginning of the relationship. It may seem hard to find the time now, but we can ask ourselves, weren't we busy when we first met? We managed to find time then. The problem is that we're no longer in that exciting, new relationship, discovery mode. We already know our partner well. We're not so curious about them, not so anxious or concerned about "winning" them over, as we once were.

We may no longer look at our partner every day with eyes of love, unless we're aware that our time together might be tragically ending. Sometimes I get an image of a desperate man, sitting at the side of his critically ill wife. Taking her hand, looking into her eyes, he is showing her his love as perhaps he hasn't since their wedding day. Their years of bickering and disappointments disappear as the two of them bask in that profound moment of intimate recognition. It is beautiful to behold.

Yet love is too important to put aside until it is too late to enjoy. Intimacy can slip away while we're not paying attention. A relationship needs to be nourished and fed with frequent experiences of intimacy.

Sometimes intimacy arises spontaneously, inspired by a romantic environment or situation. But life isn't always romantic. I can't always be with my beloved partner on a beach under a full moon, or in front of a fireplace in a luxurious five-star hotel, or wherever it is that turns us on. Even if we're at home or even in the same room at the same time, we may be individually engrossed in a hobby, a favorite TV show, cleaning out the garage, or looking at fabric samples for a new couch. We may be side by side, but we are not engaged with each other's soul.

Relationships can starve while we're looking the other way. I don't want to wait for a tragedy or a full moon to remind Richard and me of our love. I'm guessing that you feel the same way about your relationship or a relationship that you look forward to having one day.

In the beginning, not only were we motivated by wanting to know each other, but our growing intimacy was also encouraged by our internal biology. Our brains automatically produce hormones propelling us to fall in love, although this probably has more to do with the need to propagate the species than with concern about our personal happiness.

Once the togetherness of a relationship is achieved, once coupledom is arrived at, this inborn support system begins to lose steam. Or, even more troubling, our—or our partner's—biology might actually become distinctly *unhelpful* by causing a slow down of libido or a diminishing or loss of sexual response.

Richard and I—and the many couples who have attended our Intimacy Retreats—find that by consciously reminding ourselves to attend to our love, to experience our sense of "we-ness" in body, heart, and soul, our relationship stays at the top of our agenda.

Richard and I have a daily ten-minute appointment to share and enjoy sacred and intimate lovemaking. We hope this book will inspire you to do so as well.

Which brings up the question, does intimacy always imply or require sexual activity?

Does Intimacy = Sex?

No, intimacy does not require sexual activity. You can share intimacy with your best friend or even with someone who happens to sit next to you on an airplane. It is not unusual to develop feelings of intimacy with strangers during moments of heightened stress, such as being on an elevator when the power goes out, or with comrades in the action of war, or with neighbors we've never met before, when a hurricane comes calling.

You can feel joyfully intimate with your partner as you share your pride in seeing your child or grandchild take her first step or win an award. You can certainly be intimate without sexual touching. When couples' therapy is successful, it is usually because the therapist has helped facilitate an emotional experience of intimacy for the couple right there in her office.

However, sexual relations are usually an important part of having—and being—a significant other. You can watch TV or share house payments and yard work with a roommate. What most deeply defines a couple as a couple is the more private realm of physical caressing and sexual energy.

You and your partner may both want to experience intimacy but might think of it in different ways. Often, but not always, the difference is split along gender lines. Many men—including my husband—tend to think of intimacy as the *end result* of a sexual interaction. Let's have sex and we'll become intimate. Well, they probably wouldn't actually use words like *intimate* or *intimacy*.

RICHARD SAYS   *Intimacy may mean things other than sex, but for me the two have always been connected.*

Many women—including me—often prefer to establish and recognize feelings of intimacy with our partner *before* engaging in sexual interaction. Why would we want to have sex with someone we aren't already feeling close to, feeling good about? For many of us, we may sometimes even prefer, or at least prefer to start with, other aspects of intimacy, such as communication and cuddling.

Speaking of communication, this is another difference between Richard and me. He thinks that the purpose of conversation is to convey information. For me, and others with a similar temperament, it is the conversing itself, the communing, which helps create intimacy.

It may be gender-based hormones that influence our thinking and our behavior in such different ways. For example, recent research has shown that although all humans exhibit a fight-or-flight reaction to stress, women often have a third response. They call a friend; they reach out, connect, and communicate with another person.

Additional research indicates that women may have more connections and synapses between their left and right brain hemispheres than do men. Without this connection, a person finds it difficult to both feel emotion (a right brain function) and simultaneously use words to express it (a left brain function). This could certainly be an obstacle to empathic communication.

RICHARD SAYS *It is probably harder for me—and most men—to talk about feelings than it is for Diana, and most women. I don't know if it is in our DNA, our brain structure, or our upbringing, but there are clear differences in our styles of communication. Many men think that women just talk too much.*

Regardless of which partner, male or female, thinks which way, having differing viewpoints and functionality regarding intimacy, communication, and sex leads to an uncomfortable stalemate, weakens a relationship, and leaves both partners stranded on opposite sides of an ever-widening gap. The lovemaking practices presented in this book provide a way of bridging that gap.

It is amazing that maintaining intimacy, sexual or otherwise, between two people who love each other can be such a challenge. Oh, the mechanics of copulation are pretty simple to figure out. And it is usually easy for most guys to reach a "happy ending" through the thrusting motions of intercourse. We women, on the other hand, and many men as well, seem to want—and need—something more. Maybe it is just more time, or increased or different stimulation. More "outercourse." More communication. A vibrator can provide the desired sexual stimulation and also reduce the time requirement, a major issue in today's busy world. But there is still something more—an elusiveness, a mystery sometimes, not only to our enjoying orgasmic sex but also, and much more importantly, to the creating of meaningful connection through both sexual touch and verbal communication.

So how do we keep intimacy and passion alive in an ongoing, long-term relationship? How can we meet our need to be touched and loved, physically, emotionally, and spiritually? What is Tantra and how can it help?

Tantra

Thousands of years ago in India, somebody—or a group of somebodies—realized that increasing awareness of sexual energy could lead to an awakening of higher consciousness. They developed various mental and physical trainings for spiritual realization. Sometimes a partner is involved, sometimes not. These diverse teachings are collectively known as *Tantra*.

Tantra? Tantrum? A sophisticated woman overheard Richard and me talking in a restaurant. Sitting with her husband and another couple, she laughed as we walked past her and said, "Oh, I know all about sexual tantrum—it is my husband insisting, 'I want it, I want it, I want it!'"

No, Tantra is not the plural of tantrum. A Sanskrit word, *Tantra* translates to mean a "weaving," an "expansion," or a "continuum." It also refers to a set of spiritual teachings. Tantra can be thought of as a form of *yoga*, another Sanskrit word, meaning "to join." Tantra is about joining and expanding, weaving our energies, for the purpose of opening ourselves up to the entire universe.

Tantra encourages mindfulness, inviting us to live each moment with awareness. Although the true origins of Tantra are not agreed upon by all scholars and historians, the original teachings were shaped and influenced by various Hindu and Buddhist traditions. Today, they have been further expanded and reshaped by modern knowledge of psychology and a Western interest in practical application to our stressful lives.

Sometimes those who have heard of Tantra seem afraid to even acknowledge it. Perhaps they are thinking, "We aren't going to talk about *sex*, are we?" Tantra is and isn't about sex. I suppose that's like saying that a serving of escargot is and isn't about snails.

Sexuality, the most physically intimate of human interactions, is seen in Tantra as a sacred activity, continuously reenacting the original creation of the universe. Tantra lovers honor one another as divine beings. Lovemaking becomes a way to create blissful states of consciousness, to unite with one another and with the power and love of creation itself.

Tantra describes a movement of energy, a welling up within us, of joyous excitation.[1] Unlike forms of meditation that cause us to withdraw from the world of the senses, Tantra encourages us to start with the senses, building on their ability to focus us in the present moment. This energy need not be explicitly sexual. All sensual experience is appreciated as a tool for our spiritual awakening.

Tantra brings poetry to lovemaking. When Richard and I caress one another's face and our eyes meet and we breathe together and acknowledge our rising passion, sense our hearts joining and our spirits soaring, this is Tantra.

RICHARD SAYS   *Whatever you call it, it is the experience, more than the reading about the philosophy, that makes it meaningful.*

Tantra occurs only in the present moment. When I smell a rose, I smell it in this moment, not yesterday or tomorrow, but right now, right here. And if I take that rose-smelling experience into my total being, aware both of the scent and of my bodily response to the scent, aware of the softness of the petals and the awakening of rose energy in my heart, then in that moment I am open to the fullness of who I am. This is Tantra. And if Richard and I smell the rose together, and we share it as a deep inner experience, our separateness dissolves and together we experience Tantra.

At one level, tantric sex is gourmet lovemaking. It is sex slowed down, more focused, with more opportunity for a woman's pleasure, which usually means more pleasure for both lovers. At another level, it is not about copulation at all. It is about awakening the energy of life that runs through our bodies. Tantra embraces the physical as a manifestation of the divine. We discover divinity alive and vibrating within us, and we share it with our partner through sacred awareness and sexual ceremony.

Some spiritual paths teach us to deny, to say not this, not that. They teach us that we are not the body, not the mind, not our actions, not our thoughts. Stripped of what we are not, these paths allow us to see the emergence of who we may be. Tantra takes the seemingly opposite approach and teaches us to say YES! to this, YES! to that. I smell the rose and I am that experience; my lover touches me and I am that experience; there is nothing that I am not; I am everything. All experience can be a doorway to who I am, provided I focus on the experience itself by using intentional awareness.

Contrary to popular belief, Tantra was never about mastering complex sexual positions, such as those described in the *Kama Sutra*, nor was it even designed to help us improve our relationships. Its original purpose was to help practitioners connect with an inner essence of God. Yet when we use Tantric principles to experience energy, we also deepen our connection with our beloved, not just sexually but emotionally and spiritually as well. When Richard and I share this intentional awareness, our passion is renewed and love is reborn.

Tantra Tai Chi: From Martial Art to Marital Art

In China, perhaps around the same time as Tantra was being developed in India, somebody—or a group of somebodies—

realized that slow, mindful, physical movements could increase and circulate the flow of internal energy in our bodies, leading to better health and longer life. This type of solitary exercise became known as *T'ai Chi* (also spelled *Taiji*). You may have seen people performing these choreographed moves, perhaps in the early morning in a park, or in a television commercial.

T'ai Chi means the "supreme ultimate," that which is before all else and to which all returns. In addition to being practiced for health benefits, T'ai Chi is the foundation for various Chinese martial art forms. Before meeting Richard, I spent many years training in Aikido, a Japanese martial art that is based in a similar meditative energy.

After Richard and I were married, I began to hold meditation classes in our home. Richard attended. After all, they were right in our living room, and he believed that meditation was a good thing to do. However, he would inevitably fall asleep within minutes. Others had fallen asleep during these quiet meditation sessions, and I always later assured them that there was no problem, that they were probably experiencing the benefits at some level, even if they weren't aware of it. (Actually I don't know if that is true or not, but it seemed like a good response at the time. Maybe the Zen masters know better, whacking people on their backs to keep them awake.)

In my heart, I was disappointed that Richard wasn't aware of experiencing anything consciously during the meditation. I loved being conscious of energy and aware of meditative states of being, and I wanted to share those experiences with him.

And, yes, I was embarrassed, too, especially when he started to snore. This never bothered me much when it was someone other than my husband. (The same idiosyncrasy or habit exhibited by someone other than our partner is often not nearly so annoying.)

About this same time, I discovered T'ai Chi Chih, a short series of movements that are easier to learn and remember than most T'ai Chi styles, and much easier to practice than Aikido.

I invited Richard to do a few of these simple moving exercises with me. We began to practice them together. T'ai Chi Chih can quickly provide an awareness and recognition of energy in your body. One day, in the middle of doing the movements, Richard turned to me with a smile and said, "Now I know why you want me to stay awake during meditation!"

RICHARD SAYS   *It was a phenomenal "ah-ha" moment for me. Doing the movements, I found a sense of stillness that I never knew before—a calming, a place of peace and consciousness. I had had a taste of this experience some years before, trekking in the Himalayas and walking the rice fields in Bali, but I never expected it in my own living room.*

Wow! I thought, if this works for Richard, it will be great for many other people as well, especially those who fall asleep while trying to meditate. Eventually, Richard and I both became certified instructors of T'ai Chi Chih. We especially enjoyed teaching other couples to practice together. A feeling of peaceful harmony occurs when we become mindful of our bodies and aware of our energy flow. Sharing that experience with your beloved partner creates a special intimacy.

We dedicated ourselves more and more to helping couples find happiness in their relationships. A new program evolved, a partnered exercise that emphasizes sexual energy, which we named Tantra Tai Chi. Tantra Tai Chi is a modern "relationship exercise," an energy practice that blends meditative movement and internal focus with the purposeful sharing of sexual energy, creating a strong intimate and emotional connection with one's beloved partner. The principles of Tantra Tai Chi can be applied both in the exercises themselves and also in actual lovemaking.

RICHARD SAYS *Without the connection to sexual activity, my interest would probably have disappeared by now.*

Doing the exercises together provides a deepening of connection and creates an environment of intimacy. As you practice the movements described in this book, you will become engaged with the intrinsic energy of presence. Synchronizing your presence, you and your beloved will enter together into a real experience of love.

Tantra Tai Chi will change how you make love and how you use lovemaking to create intimacy.

Richard and I designed the Tantra Tai Chi program as a way to teach other couples what we have discovered in our own ongoing journey of intimacy. Knowing how to keep intimacy alive in our own relationship has kept us from getting stuck or side-tracked from our marriage vow to love one another for a whole lifetime.

The purpose of Tantra Tai Chi is to bring your mind's attention to your body's presence. When you become mentally and physically centered in your body, you become more open to a naturally joyous state of being. You enter into the "here and now," where only love is present. Past and future disappear, only the eternal moment exists. When you move into this sacred moment in the presence of your partner, you share together the love that lives within each of you. This love is a spiritual state, an expansive, inclusive experience that reaches beyond personal understanding. It can even manifest as an orgasmic void, a state beyond words or comprehension.

Throughout all the Tantra Tai Chi movements there is an emphasis on sexual energy. For example, tightening the sexual, or pubococcygeal, muscles brings your attention to this vital area of your body. The pubococcygeal, or "PC," muscles run from your pubic bone in front to the coccyx, or tailbone, in back, spanning your pelvic floor. Ancient Indian and Chinese teachings both recognized this sexual area as a gateway to powerful currents of life force that can be experienced throughout your whole body. In Tantra Tai Chi, we encourage you to become present in your *sex center*.

Connecting the Sex Center with the Heart Center

The *heart center*, located in the center of your chest, is where you experience personal emotion and compassion, as well as devotional spiritual love. When the link between the sex center and the heart center becomes activated, energy flows more freely between them. Love and sexuality become joined, giving birth to a high state of intimacy that can nourish your relationship and fulfill your soul.

This movement of energy between the sex and heart centers is the basic premise of Tantra Tai Chi. As the link between these centers strengthens, love becomes a tangible feeling within you and a spiritual opening takes place. In Tantra Tai Chi, we call the spiritual center *bindi*, and you'll learn more about this later. The exercises in this book help you focus your attention in these three primary centers: sex, heart, and bindi.

The intention of the basic Tantra Tai Chi movements is to encourage you to explore sacred intimacy. Sacred intimacy is that experience you have when you have dropped all your masks and stand revealed to one another as your authentic selves. Underneath all your pretensions and projections, you are each a beautiful being, perfect and whole. Through Tantra Tai Chi you can let go into truly being who you are, and then share your perfect presence with your beloved. This is the greatest gift you can give one another. This is the hope and promise of love.

Richard and I share sacred sexual intimacy for at least ten minutes every day. I will remind you of this over and over again.

That's not much more time than you might spend getting off the phone with someone you don't even want to be talking with. At our workshops, and in this book, we reveal the secrets and techniques we have discovered for creating and maintaining intimacy in our busy lives.

How Does Tantra Tai Chi Relate to Lovemaking?

The Tantra Tai Chi exercises teach you to bring your attention inside your body. Taking this skill into the bedroom will change forever how you make love. By focusing on the sex, heart, and bindi centers during lovemaking, you transform the paradigm of sexual activity from a direct linear release of tension (climax) to a more circular journey of bliss. You and your beloved will dance and swirl between each of the centers within your bodies.

Passion responds to an ongoing tension of separation and coming together. The early phase of dating, before living together, automatically creates this pattern. Similarly, Tantra Tai Chi provides you with positions of separation ("Solo Stillness") and togetherness (the "Connected Pose"). Also, pausing during lovemaking to consciously go within one's self, to a place of quiet stillness, and then sharing an eyes-open connection, can raise sexual activity to levels of intimacy that take you beyond yourselves into realms of unconditional ecstasy.

The easy exercises of Tantra Tai Chi—whether done naked at home or clothed at an Intimacy Retreat—help you experience the richness and rapture of your love relationship. And on a larger scale, when you and your beloved enter together into the realm of sacred intimacy, you make the reality of love more available for everyone, everywhere.

You can use Tantra Tai Chi as a prelude to sex, or to create erotic intimacy *without* actual sexual engagement. For example, there have been times when Richard would want to have sex, and I did not. He might ask me, then, if I would do a few minutes of Tantra Tai Chi with him, and I would agree; yes, I could do that. When we concluded, it would surprise me that he sometimes actually seemed quite satisfied. Apparently, a man's request for sex can really be about wanting to connect, to share love, to merge into the heart of his beloved. It doesn't always have to be a physical, sexual act.

RICHARD SAYS *It surprised me, too. Bringing the sexual energy to my heart, and feeling Diana's full attention and presence with me, is very satisfying and can be a complete experience in and of itself.*

Other times, especially if I had agreed to do Tantra Tai Chi naked, my original lack of interest might be replaced by an increasing arousal. Standing before each other, awakening and sharing our sexual, emotional, and spiritual energies, we often found a key to open the door to my desire. Or to his, if the situation were reversed. Perhaps this will happen for you as well. It is worth a try! And once you experience the essence of the Tantra

Tai Chi moves, you can easily apply them while sexually embracing your beloved.

Different Types of Sex

According to Ayurveda, an ancient Indian medical philosophy that embraces Tantra, all activities, including sex, fall into one of three categories called *gunas*. Each guna represents specific qualities, aspects, or tendencies of human nature. The three gunas are *Tama*, *Raja*, and *Sattva*. We can think of sex as being *tamasic*, *rajasic*, or *sattvic*. To appreciate how Tantra Tai Chi contributes to lovemaking, it is helpful to understand and recognize these three types of sex.

Tamasic Sex—Scratch the Itch

Sometimes sexual energy feels like an itch. With an itch comes the need to scratch it. After the scratching—which can feel really good—the itch goes away. A sexual urge can be like that. The urge is there. When I do something about it, it feels good, and then it is gone.

Or maybe it is more like an impending sneeze. There is a wonderful release as the need to sneeze intensifies and then dissipates through an explosion. And then it is over. Similar to the pressure of an itch or a sneeze, sexual urgency can lead to a welcome release. But this type of meet-the-need sex doesn't necessarily generate deep feelings of intimate bliss. It just gets the job done.

Tama, a Sanskrit word, refers to a quality of heaviness or lethargy. In food, a basic meal of meat and potatoes would be considered tamasic. Limited in pleasure and creativity, tamasic sex, like that sneeze or scratching of an itch, is at best an organic response to a biological event. Sex for the sake of sex. It is functional physical exercise that is primarily focused on the genitals. It can be quite satisfying, at least for most men. Sexual relations that are tamasic often follow a three-two-one approach to lovemaking. Three minutes of foreplay, two minutes of intercourse, and one orgasm—usually his. For women, this type of partnered sex might lead more to "bore-gasm" than orgasm. Boredom is what Alexander Pope must have recognized when he wrote, back in the eighteenth century: "She, while her Lover pants upon her breast, can mark the figures on an Indian chest."

Some of us may even fake orgasm in order to hasten the end, a deception that devalues our own right to pleasure and is strongly discouraged in tantric sex.

So often, sex in a long-term relationship does not live up to its promise at the altar. Oh sure, there may be those magical nights now and then. But as Richard and I moved further away from being newlyweds, we began to find ourselves too busy or too tired or too passionately involved with work, family responsibilities, or other activities to take the time or make the effort that magical lovemaking seemed to require. Or maybe it was because we weren't making time for each other, that we instead busied ourselves in all those other activities.

Sex became *tamasic*, less of a connection for love and more of an activity for sexual release.

RICHARD SAYS *At the time, tamasic sex was okay with me. I didn't know what I was missing.*

The urge of sexual energy can sometimes lead to sex that is not just boring but is unhealthy, negative, invasive, and more about power and control than intimacy and love. At its lowest and most reprehensible level, tamasic sex involves rape and sexual assault. One meaning of the word *tama* is "anger." At our wedding, my mother's words of wisdom were to "never go to bed angry." Good advice, although all disputes may not be able to be resolved by bedtime. However, couples who routinely express anger and rage, even if followed by hot make-up sex, can push themselves deeper into tamasic dysfunction and harm.

Tamasic sex may be abusive, barely satisfying, or just plain boring. It is probably, and unfortunately, the most common type of sexual activity in our society.

Rajasic Sex—Hot Hollywood Style

Raja refers to a quality of activity and movement. Rajasic food, for example, would be hot and spicy, like curry. Rajasic sex is passionate and energetic. Sincere effort is made to excite and pleasure one another. There may be a warm and tender connection between the lovers, with much giving and receiving. When Richard and I are rajasic in our lovemaking, we engage in both outercourse and intercourse, playfully exploring one another's bodies, kissing, touching, sucking, penetrating. Many couples use fantasy and erotica, or the stimulation of drugs or alcohol, to provide additional fuel, arousing and stirring the body through the mind.

A rajasic lover is sometimes driven by a need to prove herself or himself, enacting a desire to be a good lover. Richard and I had lots of rajasic sex in the days—and nights—of our courting. Seeing each other only occasionally added to the buildup of desire. Since our relationship was new, the challenges of conquest and seduction motivated us to exert ourselves. Love ignited us.

Once we settled in for the long haul of being life partners, those early motivations, conscious or unconscious, quietly went out the window.

All those jokes about sex after marriage, or the lack thereof, have some basis in fact. It is not that married couples don't have sex. Most do. It is just that too often the sex they do have becomes more routine than romantic. And then, after declining from romantic to routine, the sexual interludes may begin to become more rare.

Movies are filled with hot rajasic sex. Audiences enjoy the vicarious pleasure and excitement and then return home to the torpid, sluggish affair their own lovemaking has become. To bring zest back into the sexual area of their lives, some couples might experiment with "swinging" with other couples, or they might employ a little light bondage and dominance to spice things up. Infidelity—which takes a toll on intimacy—is often a search for more zest. Spice and zest are the hallmarks of rajasic sex.

Hot sex can be fun and sexually satisfying, but it does not always provide the deep, soulful nourishment we so often long for.

RICHARD SAYS *Rajasic sex can be great if we're both hot and horny at the same time.*

Sattvic Sex—Sacred Tantric Sexuality

Sattva refers to the quality of purity, a spiritual and sacred orientation. Sattvic food would be light, nothing greasy or fried. Sattvic loving is tantric sex, an experience of delicious and conscious awareness.

Sattvic sex isn't spicy. It is not "dangerous" or against society's mores. It doesn't push us to the edge and may not knock our socks off like a thrilling roller-coaster ride.

Yet the hunger for more passion, more intimacy, more *something,* can be fed with sattvic sex—not with more action, but in stillness, in quietude.

When sattvic sex takes place, there is a reversal of activity. Instead of a headlong rush toward the climactic release of orgasm, there is a continual renewal of energy circulating within and between the lovers. The timeless moment expands with unlimited boundaries, allowing a prolonged experience of delicious and conscious awareness.

There is a sweetness to this type of sex. And like a well-flavored dessert, the sweetness lasts beyond the moment, permeating the core of our being and refreshing our sense of existence. Individual satisfaction gives way to a mutual sharing of universal love. Personal pleasure is expanded to a cosmic level. Spiritual oneness prevails. Sattvic sex is calm and tranquil, and it can best be enjoyed in complete stillness. With only occasional movement to keep arousal alive, lovers embraced in sattvic sex are able to abide together in a sustained state of deep peace and love.

Sattvic sex is not divorced from the realms of tamasic and rajasic sex but rises upward from its physical roots into a rarified atmosphere of meditative surrender. Couples in a relationship that is rich in sex, love, and spirituality may find themselves moving in and out of these various qualities of sex, sometimes even during one lovemaking session.

Similarly, while the most sattvic foods are natural, raw vegetables and fruits, our diets usually include all types of food.

Sometimes Richard and I opt for the more heated and active rajasic style of lovemaking, only to find ourselves happily relaxing into the stillness of sacred sexuality the next day. Sometimes our lovemaking is a blend of active/rajasic and quiet/sattvic.

Scratching an itch brings relief. That's tamasic, restricted to the genitals. Active, fun-filled rajasic love play brings relief and also provides us with a sense of being cared for, being taken care of. Exhilarating as it is, though, rajasic sex still takes place on a personal, individual level, and at its completion can leave each of us alone with our own thoughts and emotions.

Sattvic sex opens our spiritual mind and allows us to joyfully encounter what the great teachers of meditation have written about. It is a transpersonal experience, taking us beyond our limited selves into a place where separation no longer exists. Conscious awakening into spiritual connection fulfills our innate yearning to know the truth of who we are.

RICHARD SAYS *It took me quite a while to appreciate this type of sex. I didn't get it at first. I was uncomfortable slowing down during lovemaking, afraid I'd lose my erection, my masculine prowess. Over time, I discovered that the resulting "high" of connection with Diana is a much more erotically charged experience for both of us. It goes far beyond what I had always thought of as sexual satisfaction.*

Most lovemaking tends to follow a conventional, linear pattern, starting with arousal and leading to greater and greater tension, with a final release in climax and/or ejaculation. During sattvic sex Richard and I stay relaxed, rather than tensing, even as the sexual arousal builds. Without striving or performing, we both enjoy recurring orgasms. Differing from conventional "peak" orgasms, in Tantra these are called "valley" orgasms. Paul Pearsall, author of *Super Marital Sex*, calls these experiences "psychasms." Richard and I call them lovegasms.

Think of it this way: Conventional sex might take us straight up a 1,000-foot mountain before our energy reaches the peak where he explodes, usually ending the lovemaking session. With sattvic sex, we might have our first lovegasm at 500 feet, with no explosion. We settle into it, hang out there, and build a "base camp" while we abide together in the bliss. In Sanskrit, the word for bliss is *ananda*. Ananda describes not a bungee-jumping kind of mind-blowing bliss, but an inner experience of exquisite joy.

The lovemaking doesn't end there. We can continue to ascend the mountain, having valley orgasms and hanging out in bliss at successively higher base camps. Instead of only getting to 1,000 feet, we may reach 5,000, 10,000, or 20,000 feet before peaking, if we wish, and ending the lovemaking session.

Orgasm is not the same as ejaculation. Although they usually happen at the same time, orgasm is much more than a *tamasic* sneeze in the groin. Beyond the muscular contractions and physical release, orgasm describes those wonderful liberating feelings that propel us into a sense of connection with something even beyond our bodies.

Tantra Tai Chi provides a pattern, based on three primary energy centers, that helps you enter into *sattvic* sex and the sharing of ecstasy and bliss that this type of lovemaking brings about. Tantra Tai Chi is a way of learning how to make sensual, sacred love, expanding and prolonging joyous orgasmic energy. Taking only ten minutes a day to explore the concepts and practices in this book, you can develop a deepened level of lifetime passion with your beloved.

Energy Centers in Tantra Tai Chi

There are particular areas in our bodies that are said to collect energy and to vibrate in association with specific psychospiritual qualities or circumstances. Whether real or symbolic, numerous systems of thought describe similar locations in our bodies. In Tantra, each center is called a *chakra*, meaning "wheel." Although there are also chakras in our hands, feet, and elsewhere, the seven major chakras are aligned along the torso. Taoism, which originated in China, speaks of upper, middle, and lower *dantiens*, or "fields of elixir." Kabbalah, Jewish mysticism, describes the human body itself as the microcosm of the universe, and visualizes ten *sephirot*, or spheres, each housing certain godlike qualities.

Although chakras, dantiens, and sephirot differ in language and description, they are located in similar areas on our bodies, mostly along or related to the central channel of our spinal column. This alone, regardless of the varied metaphysical explanations offered by the different systems, provides us with a useful pattern for aligning with our bodies and establishing a resonating intimacy with our partner.

Long ago, a Tai Chi master wrote that if one could visualize the spine as a string of pearls hanging down from the head, and if one could become fully present at each and every vertebra, or pearl, along that string, one would experience enlightenment. Bringing our attention, our awareness, to the energy of our spine, is clearly a pathway to spiritual vibration.

Tantra Tai Chi uses a trilogy of energy centers in the body. By naming and tapping into the energies and potential power of each of these three centers, and moving energy among them, we ceremonially and lovingly honor ourselves and one another.

The three centers in Tantra Tai Chi are related to sex, heart, and spirit. Linking these together is an invisible but tangible energy that runs throughout our bodies. A bio-electric force, it is called *qi* (pronounced "chi") in Chinese, as in *qigong* (Chi Kung). In Japanese, it is *ki*, as in Aikido. In yoga, when it is associated with the breath, it is called *prana*. In Tantra, it is said to be coiled at the base of the spine and is called *Kundalini*. It may also be considered to be the breath of the Holy Spirit, as described by Christian mystics. Different words, different descriptions, but similar experiences.

As we embrace this energy within ourselves, as we share and synchronize it with our partner, we enter into a dance of divine delight. Richard and I do this both during the actual Tantra Tai Chi exercises, and, even more intimately, during our lovemaking.

RICHARD SAYS *There are other ways to become aware of energy in the body, but I have found that practicing during sex is the most fun and fulfilling.*

Feeling Energy

Although energy is invisible, it has substance and can be felt. If this is a new concept for you, try the following exercise. (Read the description and then put the book down to try it.) Hold your hands about two feet apart, palms facing each other, and slowly move your palms toward and away from each other (see Figure 1.1 below). You can do this alone or with your partner.

You might experience energy as heat or as a magnetic pull or just as a vague sense of something that occurs as a result of the attraction between the palms. If you think you're making up whatever it is you're feeling—that's it! Our rational minds don't always accept what our body tells us.

When you do the Tantra Tai Chi movements, you may notice a tingling in your hands, or they may feel warm. This is a sign of the energy building and moving. As you continue, you may experience a transcendent, spacious, timeless feeling. You may notice feelings of love. Whatever you notice, if anything,

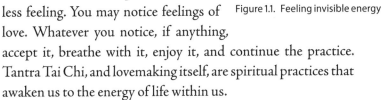

Figure 1.1. Feeling invisible energy

accept it, breathe with it, enjoy it, and continue the practice. Tantra Tai Chi, and lovemaking itself, are spiritual practices that awaken us to the energy of life within us.

Creating a Sanctuary for Love

Tantric ceremony is always best practiced in a location without distractions or interruptions. Also, while some of the Tantra Tai

Chi exercises can be comfortably performed in a public space, you will most likely want privacy for the more sexual aspects of these exercises.

You can create a private sanctuary by simply locking the door to your bedroom, closing the curtains, and turning off the TV and telephone. If there are children in the house, arranging for a regularly scheduled love time will help you set boundaries and teach them about privacy. Sharing this time together, even if it is only for ten minutes, will make your relationship be a model of love for your children. Of course, no matter how well you plan it, interruptions can—and will—occur. So be sure to keep a sense of humor in your sacred space!

Your sacred space is where you can find yourself again and again.

JOSEPH CAMPBELL, American author on the subjects of mythology and religion

You might enhance the space with beautiful pillows, incense, flower arrangements, or candles. Objects, mementos, and meaningful photos can be used to decorate and bring beauty into your sacred space. Carefully selected music can provide the perfect ambience. You might want to create a treasure box where you keep a collection of sensual items to be used only for your loving times together. Let your creativity and personal interests guide you.

Having a place in your home that can be set aside and kept sacred only for lovemaking can add a special element to your experiences. However, you can simply designate your bed or a rug as your sacred space. It is not the space itself that matters, but what you do within that space.

Some aspects of creating a sanctuary can in themselves become a ritual, such as lighting a candle to signify the beginning of your time together. In Native American ceremonies, dried sage is burned. The smoke is used to "smudge" the participants and the environment, clearing out negative energies, preparing the space for positive experiences.

> *Our most life-changing experiences take place in the bedroom.*
> JON ROBERTSON, author of *The Sacred Bedroom*

Feng shui (pronounced "fung SHWAY") is an ancient Chinese art that focuses on the arrangement of space to create harmony and success. Appropriate feng shui exists not only for physical areas but for individuals as well. For example, some directions are considered better or luckier than others for the positioning of your front door. Similarly, if you sit at a desk all day long, you would certainly want to be facing one of your better directions, which can be determined by a feng shui practitioner based on your year of birth.

But what happens when you and your partner ceremonially face each other, as in tantric sex? What if you and your partner's best and worst directions are in conflict? Richard and I asked Jami Lin, an internationally renowned feng shui master, to help us determine the most favorable direction for each of us to position ourselves in while facing one another.

Richard and I now begin and end our short, daily ceremony of tantric sex by facing each other in our best directions, according to the table that Lin developed (see the next page). I don't know whether our lives—or our loving—would be any less wonderful if we didn't arrange ourselves in this way, but it has become an integral part of our ritual. It brings a feeling of sacredness to our sanctuary.

Finding Your Best Directions

First, use the table below to determine your own and your beloved's elements, which are based on your birth years. (Note: If a birthday is before February 5, use the prior year to align with the Chinese calendar.)

Determining Your Best Directions

Year	Male	Female	Year	Male	Female	Year	Male	Female
1925	wood	wood	1943	wood	wood	1961	wood	wood
1926	earth	wood	1944	earth	wood	1962	earth	wood
1927	water	earth	1945	water	earth	1963	water	earth
1928	fire	metal	1946	fire	metal	1964	fire	metal
1929	earth	metal	1947	earth	metal	1965	earth	metal
1930	metal	earth	1948	metal	earth	1966	metal	earth
1931	metal	fire	1949	metal	fire	1967	metal	fire
1932	earth	water	1950	earth	water	1968	earth	water
1933	wood	earth	1951	wood	earth	1969	wood	earth
1934	wood	wood	1952	wood	wood	1970	wood	wood
1935	earth	wood	1953	earth	wood	1971	earth	wood
1936	water	earth	1954	water	earth	1972	water	earth
1937	fire	metal	1955	fire	metal	1973	fire	metal
1938	earth	metal	1956	earth	metal	1974	earth	metal
1939	metal	earth	1957	metal	earth	1975	metal	earth
1940	metal	fire	1958	metal	fire	1976	metal	fire
1941	earth	water	1959	earth	water	1977	earth	water
1942	wood	earth	1960	wood	earth	1978	wood	earth

(cont'd.)

Determining Your Best Directions (cont'd.)

Year	Male	Female	Year	Male	Female	Year	Male	Female
1979	wood	wood	1987	wood	earth	1995	earth	water
1980	earth	wood	1988	wood	wood	1996	wood	earth
1981	water	earth	1989	earth	wood	1997	wood	wood
1982	fire	metal	1990	water	earth	1998	earth	wood
1983	earth	metal	1991	fire	metal	1999	water	earth
1984	metal	earth	1992	earth	metal	2000	fire	metal
1985	metal	fire	1993	metal	earth			
1986	earth	water	1994	metal	fire			

Once you know what element is associated with your own and your partner's birth years, you can arrange yourselves as follows:

❄ If you were *both* born in earth or metal years, one person faces northeast, the other southwest. It doesn't matter who faces which of the two directions, and you can alternate them if you like.

❄ If you were *both* born in water, wood, or fire years, one faces north, the other south. Again, it doesn't matter which person faces north and which one faces south.

❄ *Otherwise*, the person whose element is earth or metal faces west and the one whose element is water, wood, or fire faces east.

Chapter Note

1. Portions of this section were previously published in *Ayurvedic Remedies for the Whole Family*, by Dr. Light Miller. Used by permission of the author.

Tantra Tai Chi

The exercises of Tantra Tai Chi will help you and your beloved enter into the present moment, the "now," with each other. It is only in the present moment, only in the now, that intimacy can be truly shared. Your body is always right here, right now. Tantra Tai Chi helps you take up residence in your body.

The movements are easy to do and take only a little time. You can do them clothed or naked. You can do just one of them, any one, or all of the ones presented in this book. They may seem silly at first, and you and your partner might giggle a lot. That's okay! Take it at your own pace. Don't worry about performing them perfectly. Do them your own way; make them your own. If your partner doesn't seem to understand the instructions in the same way you do, try it his or her way rather than making your partner out to be wrong.

You can use Tantra Tai Chi as a way to experience intimate connection, to initiate sexual time together, or as warm-up practice and training for the lovemaking ceremonies included in this book. The exercises are intended to bring peace, harmony, and passion to your relationship.

No Partner?

If you are practicing Tantra Tai Chi alone, you can simply imagine someone in front of you. Or you can stand before a tree. A tree is full of life and is definitely rooted in the ground, so it can be a perfect partner to connect with. For an even deeper personal experience, practice Tantra Tai Chi with yourself in front of a mirror. The eyes-open exercises will be a real eye-opener, as you begin to truly see yourself as the divine being that you are.

Then, when you do have a partner, you will have something delicious to introduce that partner to.

Partner Not Interested?

What if you are drawn to learning about the practice and philosophy of tantric sexuality but your partner won't read a book or attend a workshop? Could it be that your partner is interested in sex but not in some program that sounds a little far-out, esoteric, or New Agey? As you read this book, you'll discover that being intimately present with your partner is very practical and down-to-earth. You'll be able to take some small part of what you learn and find a way to apply it in your relationship, to share it, even if it is not initially your partner's cup of tea. Just a few moments of true intimate connection can make a huge difference and can indeed be transformational.

Is your partner not interested in sexual activity at all? Perhaps you can let him or her know how important it is to you, that you have discovered a whole new way of thinking about sex. It is generally advised that conversations about sex should take place outside of the bedroom, not in the middle of the activity itself. If you're not currently engaging in sex with your partner, that's your only choice anyway. However, if you do have sexual times together, you might try influencing the shape of those sessions by guiding your partner to touch you or look at you, or to be with you in ways that can create an opening for deeper intimacy and more pleasure. Afterward, be sure to let your partner know how wonderful the experience has been for you.

It takes courage to be truthful. It is often easier to let things be, to not rock the boat, to let things continue as they are. If you are yearning for more intimacy in your relationship, a little boat-rocking might be a good idea. Perhaps your partner is just waiting for you to lead the way. I encourage you to lead gently, without laying blame or criticism upon your partner, or upon yourself.

I can't say it will be easy. Sexual intimacy is so often permeated with disappointments and frustrations. Richard and I have had our share of both. Remember, it helps to have a good sense of humor.

The process of maturing into a higher level of love is an ongoing journey of self-growth that can be challenging yet profoundly rewarding.

RICHARD SAYS *When Diana first suggested a new approach to our sexuality, my ego was crushed. I was understandably hesitant. But the twin rewards of making her happy and maybe even having more—or better—sex were the carrots that kept me going forward.*

Solo Stillness

Solo Stillness is the opening, the starting point of Tantra Tai Chi. It is a nonmoving position that creates a separate space for each of you in the midst of your togetherness. Solo Stillness invites you into the silence of your own being and gives outward configuration to your inner self. If you meditate, or do yoga, you will recognize some aspects of this quiet, standing pose.

When you practice Tantra Tai Chi with your partner, this is your alone time. Alone time is necessary in a relationship. You must take time to stand on your own feet, to breathe your own breath, to create space between the two of you. Although you are in front of one another, Solo Stillness encourages you to separate, to step back from the shared oneness into your own individual connection with that oneness.

Solo Stillness is your private time, allowing you to refuel from the unlimited wellspring of universal energy. This simple posture creates a safe, strong home base for your journey into intimacy. When you stand in Solo Stillness, you temporarily remove yourself from being available to others. You are alone with yourself, not presently needed by anyone else. For this moment, there is only you and your connection to your own spiritual source.

You may take to Solo Stillness like a duck to water, delighting so intensely in your own sense of self that you almost forget about your partner. Or you may find this pose challenging. You may feel uncomfortable in the unfamiliarity of your own being. We are rarely taught to cherish ourselves in this way, to commune with our own hearts, to be this intimate with ourselves.

Let there be spaces in your togetherness. And let the winds of the heavens dance between you.
KAHLIL GIBRAN,
The Prophet

The more you practice Solo Stillness, the more familiar and comfortable the position will become. Eventually it may remind you of a favorite chair, something you sink into with contentment and ease.

In Tantra Tai Chi, and in life, Solo Stillness represents the place you come from and to which you return. When you nurture yourself, you have more to offer your partner. When you tend to your individual spiritual connection, you bring that greater sense of yourself to share with your beloved.

Lovemaking is an experience of giving and receiving. Solo Stillness prepares you for the fullness of being a receiver. It teaches you how to relax into your own body without having to check whether it is okay with anyone else. In Solo Stillness, you let go of having to please anyone else, you let go of the need to perform or even to relate to your partner at all. It is important to create a place in your life—and in your lovemaking—for this inward turning. It is not selfish in a negative sense; rather it is *self*-ish in the sense of caring for one's self, for one's soul.

Solo Stillness is a gift you give to yourself. It is your personal connection with the most inner part of your soul, that real but invisible part of you that cannot be seen with the human eye, cannot be burned with fire, cannot be made wet with water. In Solo Stillness, you affirm your connection with this enduring and undying self. You stand firmly and fearlessly on the surface of the planet, absorbing earth's energy through your feet.

I have a real problem with stillness. With just stopping and being quiet.
GILLIAN ANDERSON, actress, *The X-Files*

In Solo Stillness, you stand comfortably relaxed, assured of your place in the universe. In the presence of your partner, you stand in the midst of your own love.

Sole Mates/Soul Mates
A connection with the earth is vital to the practice of Tantra Tai Chi, and to life itself. The earth is a potent storehouse of rich magnetic power. Guide yourself in Solo Stillness to be aware of the soles of your feet. You can think of yourself and your beloved as "sole mates," as well as "soul mates." Both of you will be making a connection down into the earth from the bottoms of your feet. You can imagine that you have your own roots going down, and that your partner has roots also going down into the same rich

earth. This will give you a strong base, a support system that will ground you even as you open yourself up to higher frequencies of energy and love.

RICHARD SAYS *I like to curl my toes against the floor; it helps me get in touch with the earth. I don't feel those imaginary roots as easily as Diana does. But we are definitely "sole" mates, since our feet are exactly the same length!*

How to Do Solo Stillness

- ❖ Each partner stands in his or her own space, facing each other, about two feet apart from one another, positioned in your best directions (see table on page 40).

- ❖ Place your feet directly under your own hips, with your toes pointed forward and planted in a relaxed way. Let your weight be evenly distributed on both feet.

- ❖ Let your knees relax and bend slightly, gradually lowering your waist.

- ❖ Feel as if you are resting on your hips.

- ❖ Leaving your shoulders and arms relaxed, raise your hands in front of you, palms down, until they are just below your waist, fingers pointing forward toward your partner (see Figure 2.1 on the next page).

- ❖ Let your eyes close.

- ❖ Direct your awareness to the bottoms of your feet.

- ❖ Feel how your feet and legs are supporting you.

❁ Sense the hardness—or softness—
  of the surface on which you are
  standing.

❁ Imagine that you can feel
  roots extending from the
  bottoms of your feet down
  into the earth.

❁ Breathe.

How Long to Stay
in Solo Stillness?

You can enjoy Solo Stillness for
as long a period of time as you like.
This is, in essence, a meditation position. However, when practicing with a

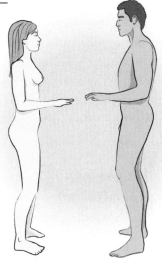

Figure 2.1. Solo Stillness

partner you may only want to remain in Solo
Stillness for a period of three or four long breaths to begin with.
When you have a sense of connecting with your own self, allow
your eyes to open.

If your eyes open first, hold your gaze softly on your beloved's
face so you will be there when his or her eyes open to meet yours.
If you feel uncomfortable waiting, or restless, softly say the word
"eyes" as an invitation for your partner to join you.

You will be returning to Solo Stillness after each of the Tantra
Tai Chi movements described in this book. Every time you enter
into Solo Stillness, you will have the opportunity to experience

yourself in a new way. You might find your feet more quickly or sense your roots more deeply. You might be more aware of your body, your hands, or your breath. You might be more aware of the quiet, the stillness, the moment itself. Take time to appreciate each new version of yourself.

As a partnered practice, whatever feels right to the two of you is right enough. There is no universally "right" way to enjoy and benefit from Tantra Tai Chi or tantric sex.

Can't Stand?
Tantra Tai Chi is generally done standing, facing your partner. If standing is uncomfortable for either or both of you, you can do Solo Stillness—and all of the following Tantra Tai Chi moves—while sitting in chairs. Put your feet flat on the floor in front of your chair. Focus on feeling a connection to the earth through your sitting bones. Adapt the movements for your own comfort and pleasure.

Solo Stillness During Lovemaking
During your next time of lovemaking, invite your partner to join you in an experience of Solo Stillness—without standing in the actual Solo Stillness position. Become still. While taking a break from whatever sexual activity you were engaged in, each of you can close your eyes and settle quietly into yourself while continuing to maintain physical contact with the other. After a few breaths, open your eyes. Behold your beloved! You may say the word "eyes" as an invitation for your partner to join you.

This momentary break from your normal pattern will shift your sexual experience into a new level of lovemaking.

Sometimes I feel disconnected from Richard or my attention wanders in the midst of making love. To regain that all-important connection, I ask for Solo Stillness. Reconnecting with myself, I am again ready to join with him.

Connected Pose

After Solo Stillness, when you and your partner have opened your eyes, you will be ready to move into the *Connected Pose*. You will step out of your own private meditative space into a face-to-face engagement with your partner. Without physical contact, yet more powerful than a hug, Connected Pose always follows Solo Stillness.

They do not love that do not show their love.
WILLIAM SHAKESPEARE,
Two Gentlemen of Verona

Relationship is all about engagement. After over twenty-three years of marriage, Richard and I still prefer to think of ourselves as "engaged." Too often, marriage is considered something that is finalized at a wedding, ending an engagement. Instead, marriage might be better defined as a commitment to stay engaged.

In Connected Pose, you will stand facing each other, relaxed, with arms open to receive and share. There is nothing present but the two of you, and the energy you bring to this encounter. It is a vulnerable position. There is nowhere to hide, no way of avoiding one another's presence. You are opening yourselves to a connection that goes beyond the physical, into the core of your being.

If I had to pick only one thing for you to share with your partner about Tantra Tai Chi, it would be the Connected Pose.

Eye Contact

Eye contact, for those of us blessed to have eyesight, is a key component of tantric sexuality. Eye contact inspires trust. By allowing your partner to see you, you reveal your soul. Intimacy can be thought of as "into-me-see." This profound experience of intimacy, of connection, takes place only in the present moment. When you look into your beloved's eyes, that moment is highlighted and brought into sharper focus. Eye contact increases the flow of intimate energy. You are reminded of your love. By maintaining eye contact with your partner, you may find yourself expanding into a deeper presence with one another.

It all comes down to presence. Being present in the moment. And love.
BHAGAVAN DAS,
Western yogi,
singer, teacher

Eye contact is not always comfortable at first, and it often takes some getting used to. Although Richard is very visually oriented, he didn't make eye contact easily for the first seven years we were together. At a restaurant, his eyes would wander around, looking at the servers, the other diners, the wall décor. Often I would complain or ask him what he was looking at. Neither approach was helpful in bringing his attention back to me. Complaining never helps. If I asked him what he had been looking at, he usually didn't know. Trying to remember, he would then become even further distanced from his body, his presence, and our connection.

After he discovered the delights of making eye contact, he taught me to say, "Eyes" to him instead of complaining or asking him where he was. This simple reminder brings him back to the present moment, which is where we both want to be.

Sexual activity is often relegated to the dark—lights out, eyes closed. Although such anonymity can sometimes contribute to steamy sex, eye contact supports the connection you yearn for.

RICHARD SAYS *Making love with the lights on and our eyes open has enabled me to have an intimate connection with Diana that I had never imagined possible. Believe it or not, I've even interrupted her oral pleasuring of me to ask for eye contact.*

When you are seen in this moment-to-moment intimate way, you know yourself to be alive. For this moment, you are free from any other needs, desires, conflicts, or questions. You are present with your beloved in your own wholeness. This is the gift of the eyes-open Connected Pose.

I Am Here

Words matter. Words can create intimacy or derail it. Words can be used to express presence. In Connected Pose, you will say to each other three simple words: "I am here." Often said at times of crisis, to let our loved one know we are there, these words call up a powerful image of urgency and importance. A life-threatening situation jolts us into remembering and announcing our love. "I am here," we say. "I am here with you, you are not alone. I offer you the strength and presence of my love. I am here."

How much more wonderful to give this verbal gift to each other when there is no emergency, no tragic circumstance, no one being rushed off in an ambulance.

The phrase, "I am here," is found in the Bible, in Hebrew, as *hineni* ("hee-NAY-nee"). When Moses stands beside the Burning Bush, a voice calls out, "Moses, where are you?" "*Hineni*," Moses answers. "I am here." More than just a statement of location or a simple response to a roll call in school, "hineni" means: "I am here, I am attentive to you and alert to our relationship." To say, "Hineni" or to say, "I am here" is to honor your beloved with your mindful presence.

When I say these words to Richard, in Connected Pose or at any other time, for that moment, I am right here with him. I am available, I am in present time and space and nowhere else. My thoughts, my whole being, my physical body, my emotional self, all of me is here. I am here, with all my *mishigas*—my craziness, my stories, my good and bad personality traits, and everything that makes up who I am. For this moment, I am here. Even if you never do any of the exercises in this book, I hope you will find a way for you and your partner to show up for each other in the simplicity of this authentic presence.

How to Do Connected Pose

❖ Begin in Solo Stillness (see page 48).

❖ Allow your eyes to open. Gaze at your beloved without staring, using a soft-eye focus. Allow your partner to see into you. Intimacy = into-me-see. If your eyes open first, hold your gaze on your partner's face until both of you have made eye contact.

❖ Together, widen your stance by moving one foot out to the side. The female partner steps sideways to the left, the male partner steps to the right.

❖ As you step sideways, let your hands drop down and out to your sides, palms facing toward your partner (see Figure 2.2).

❖ Continue to hold eye contact, and say, "I am here" to one another.

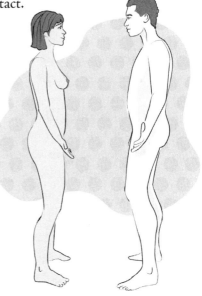

Figure 2.2. Connected Pose

Male-Female Polarity

Regardless of our sexual orientation, we each have both masculine and feminine aspects within us. Balancing and aligning your individual male-female polarity is one of the principles of tantric sex. The right side of the body is said to be the masculine side; the left side, the feminine. In Tantra Tai Chi, to step sideways into Connected Pose, you first shift your weight onto the foot opposite to the direction you'll be moving.

To move to the left, I first shift my weight onto my right foot, connecting briefly with my "inner male." Then stepping out to the left, I move into full acceptance of my femininity.

Richard does the opposite. By shifting weight first to his left foot, he touches base with his "inner female." Stepping fully to the right, he accepts and steps into his full masculinity.

Thus we each become whole unto ourselves.

RICHARD SAYS　*Aside from this philosophical story, and maybe more important, is that by my stepping sideways to the right and Diana stepping to the left, we end up moving in the same direction.*

Combining Solo Stillness and Connected Pose

Practice moving between Solo Stillness and Connected Pose, staying in each for at least fifteen seconds. After each of the subsequent movements of Tantra Tai Chi, you will return to Solo Stillness and then to Connected Pose.

If you have only a few moments in which to connect with each other, you can do Solo Stillness and Connected Pose. And if time is really short, Connected Pose alone can be a touchstone that centers the two of you in a moment of conscious relationship, providing a reminder to each of you that you are indeed lovers.

Richard and I intentionally enjoy connection through sexual intimacy every day. But sometimes we miss our daily ten-minute practice. On such a day, we may later find ourselves heading out for a busy social evening with friends. We're not a couple who sticks together all evening at a party, so there isn't likely to be much togetherness once we get there. Before we leave the house, we'll often stop and do the Connected Pose in order to purposefully reestablish the energy of our love. Only one of us has to remember to do so and to invite the other to join. It doesn't matter who remembers first. Relationships are teamwork. The roles we play may change from time to time. What's important is to find a way of establishing a connection—and reestablishing it—every day. This simple position, Connected Pose, can do that for you.

Restore Harmony with the Connected Pose

You don't always have to feel good about each other before engaging in tantric sex or doing Tantra Tai Chi. In fact, if Richard and I find ourselves out of sorts with one another, we will do Solo Stillness and Connected Pose to restore harmony. We go back and forth, separating and joining, even when we least feel like it. Before we had a commitment to use Tantra Tai Chi in this way, an argument or upset could literally affect us for days. I might have tried to get Richard to *talk more* about the issue, which would usually shut him down even more. There's been a lot of learning over the years of our relationship, both individually and as a couple. But, more than anything else, we have found that this simple exercise, done in silence, helps each of us regain sanity and perspective, together. That's the key point, doing it together. In the past, Richard might have left the house for a while, removing himself from the stressful situation, and I might have meditated to do the same. Such strategies were personally helpful, and eventually we would reconnect.

Tantra Tai Chi gives us a way to speed up this process. We stand in front of each other and close our eyes, settling into Solo Stillness. If I am agitated, I can't easily relax and I will open my eyes very quickly. Instead of feeling my feet connected to the ground, I am up in my head, thinking about the issue that annoyed me. (And probably assigning blame to Richard!) When our eyes open, we step together, sideways, into Connected Pose. Since I am probably still annoyed, I will not enjoy looking at Richard and will want to hurry up and get back to Solo Stillness. I symbolically move away from him, although remaining right in front of him. We are doing the moves but not yet connecting.

We may do this a number of times, moving between Solo Stillness (eyes closed) and Connected Pose (eye contact). Each time I return to Solo Stillness, I settle a little bit more into my own body. As I become aware of my feet, my roots, I start to appreciate my own inner presence. At first I might resist this appreciative feeling, because something in me wants to hold on to being right, even at the expense of acknowledging my own aliveness. Eventually, as I become more accepting of myself, I can more easily accept Richard's presence across from me in Connected Pose.

As we continue, harmony is restored and love is remembered and restored in our bodies. The issue at hand may not be resolved, but we will have reestablished that our love is more important than any issue. I know a shift has occurred when upon opening my eyes I am happy to see him. Only then can I truly say, "I am here."

RICHARD SAYS *In the past, when conflict arose between us, I would usually disappear—both physically and emotionally. I could spend a day or two feeling withdrawn, making matters worse, and feeling terrible about the whole situation. Using Solo Stillness and Connected Pose gives me a way to calm myself without going anywhere. As we go back and forth between the positions, I ask myself, "Would I rather be right or would I rather be happy?" Although I'd probably prefer to be both right and happy, it doesn't take too long before happiness wins out.*

How Long to Stay in Connected Pose?

You can stay in Connected Pose as long as you both enjoy the sense of being connected. If you know other Tantra Tai Chi moves, you can continue from here, or you can end the session with a ceremonial bow (see the next page).

Namasté—The Bow

If you've ever been to a yoga class, you have probably experienced *namasté* (pronounced "nah-MAH-stay"), the ceremonial bow also commonly used as a greeting or parting gesture in India.

In Japan, the art of bowing is called *gassho* and signifies the oneness of Buddha and all beings. There is an entire Buddhist practice of performing hundreds—even thousands—of bows each day. In Aikido and other martial arts, practitioners bow before getting on and off the mat. We bow in appreciation to the teacher and to our partners before and after training together. In Zen meditation, we sit on cushions, often facing the wall. The meditator bows toward her cushion before sitting down and again when leaving, and she joins in bowing when another meditator prepares to sit next to her. In many other spiritual practices, too, a bow signifies the deepest respect.

> *Namasté means… "I honor the place in you in which the entire universe resides. I honor the place in you of love, of light, of truth, and of peace. I honor the place within you where if you are in that place in you, and I am in that place in me, there is only one of us."*
>
> RAM DASS, spiritual teacher and author of *Be Here Now*

A specific placement of hands can have a direct influence on our mind and psyche. Such hand positions are called *mudra* (pronounced "moo-DRAH"). Bringing your hands together at your heart, palm to palm, bowing with reverence and respect, creates an entirely different feeling than, for example, balling up your hands into fists, which stimulates aggression. It is much more difficult to express or feel anger when your hands are touching your heart and are held in a prayer position. The hand position itself creates a sense of calmness and peace.

As Westerners, although we may incline our bodies or bow our heads in religious settings, our way of greeting or taking leave of someone is to wave, hug, or shake hands. The closest we come to a bow is sometimes a slight nod of the head. The unfamiliarity of bowing therefore heightens its ritual value for us, creating a sense of sacredness and ceremony.

Bowing is a very serious practice. You should be prepared to bow even in your last moment; when you cannot do anything except bow, you should do it.
SUZUKI ROSHI,
Zen Mind, Beginners Mind

Ceremony coaxes us into the best of ourselves. It emphasizes the importance of an occasion, showing that we take it seriously. Ceremony bestows honor, simply by the attention given to that being honored. Even at a casual birthday party, when the candles on the cake are lit, the hubbub and chatter ceases, and quiet, loving attention is given to the birthday person.

Ceremony can be used to turn ordinary time into sacred, intimate time. Tantra Tai Chi is a ceremony, a ritual. After doing Tantra Tai Chi together, and also whenever we end a lovemaking session, whether it has been tantric or not, Richard and I bow to each other. Although we don't stand up in this Tantra Tai Chi format, we do disentangle ourselves, separate from our embrace, and bow. We give each other a namasté heart salutation with respect, honor, gratitude, and joyous devotion. The act itself provides a clearly defined moment of centering into the here-and-now, which is where love itself exists.

RICHARD SAYS *The namasté bow after our lovemaking is very special. It reminds me to honor Diana and not take her or our relationship for granted. I need physical reminders like this.*

How to Do Namasté

- ❀ Begin in Solo Stillness (see page 48).

- ❀ Open your eyes, and move together into Connected Pose (see page 55).

- ❀ From Connected Pose, bring your foot back, as if returning to Solo Stillness, so both feet are directly under your hips.

- ❀ Place your hands in prayer position, palm to palm, with the sides of your thumbs touching the center of your chest and fingers pointing upward. Extend your elbows out to the sides.

- ❀ Honor each other by slowly inclining the upper part of your bodies toward one another (see Figure 2.3).

- ❀ As you bow, continue to maintain eye contact with your beloved.

Figure 2.3. Namasté bow

The Sex Center

Sex has its own energy and defines us in more ways than we are aware of. We are drawn to it, hide from it, run from it, obsess over it, fear it, love it, crave it, suppress it, chase it, and, in the end, know very little about it. What is sex and what is its hold on us, this mysterious force that rises within us and demands such attention?

This vibrant, pulsating part of ourselves is a homing signal, guiding us into our core reality, our essential self. When we allow sexual energy to awaken in us, we feel exuberant, alive, ecstatic.

Sex is a small word with lots of different meanings. Clinically, it is used to denote gender. Most often, it is a shorthand reference to intercourse, as in "we had sex." Funny how the word is used as a noun to describe something that's not really a thing at all. Even more odd, perhaps, is that sex is so often thought to mean only intercourse, a very misleading notion.

When Richard and I first published a video of our Tantra Tai Chi program, my mother watched it and said, "It is very nice, but do you have to say the word 'sex' so often?" "Yes," I replied, "someone has to."

Sex is not the answer. Sex is the question. Yes! is the answer.
AUTHOR UNKNOWN

S.E.X. = Synchronized Energy eXchange

A great way to think of the word *sex* is as an acronym for the phrase **S**ynchronized **E**nergy e**X**change—S.E.X. When partnered sexual activity is at its best, there is a sharing, an exchanging of energy. When we synchronize our energy presence with our beloved, we can become intimate beyond the definition of words. When we expand our understanding of what sex might be, we embark on a lifelong exploration and appreciation of this creative energy within us.

Sex Center

The word *sex* also identifies that private, physical area of the body. In Tantra Tai Chi, we call this your sex center. The sex center includes the entire pelvic region, your sexual and reproductive organs, and also thighs, belly, hips, and buttocks. For the purposes of Tantra Tai Chi, the whole physical and energy area below your waist falls into the sex center.

Sexual energy is the creative energy of the universe.
DEEPAK CHOPRA, MD, author of *The Path to Love*

Regardless of our relationship with sex, most of us spend the majority of our time up in our heads—a long way from the sex center. We're thinking, analyzing, judging, commenting. You may have heard that the brain is our largest sex organ. However, to enjoy full-bodied intimacy, the kind of intimacy that great lovers share, we need to become present in the fullness of our bodies. The first and second chakras, and the lower dantien, are all located in the sex center. The first, or root chakra, is at the very base of our spine. This chakra is fueled by raw sexual energy, the creative force of the universe. When our root chakra is open and flowing, we are in touch with all the earth has to offer; we feel safe and sufficient. We are comfortable with the generosity of the planet.

We are confident that our basic needs will always be met—our need for shelter, for food, and for sex. The second chakra governs the reproductive organs, and when this chakra is open and flowing, we are even more in touch with our sexuality and our creative power.

As I have mentioned, the development of Tantra Tai Chi, the use of ritual, ceremony, and energy awareness to enhance love, was supported by my many years of training in Aikido. Martial arts training always emphasizes the legs and lower part of the body. No, we don't talk about sex on the Aikido mat. It is a martial art, not a *marital* art! However, we do focus our attention below the waist. We are instructed to be mindful of our feet, to feel connected to the ground. We focus on the *hara*, a Japanese word describing a power point or center of gravity in the abdomen. We stay in touch with our hara while receiving—and redirecting—an attacker's energy. Dropping into the lower area of our body gives us strength and opens us to the infinite energy of a harmonious universe.

This martial arts focus in the belly is one way to get us out of our head and into our body. Another way, more specifically related to the art of *marital* relations, is to include the genitals themselves, to focus on the whole sex center. To engage in the practice of Tantra Tai Chi, or tantric sexuality, you don't have to start out feeling sexy or even have a desire for sex. The secret is to bring attention and energy to your sex center—lots of attention, lots of energy.

Down There

There are many words in every language for the genitals, over a thousand in English alone. Unfortunately, a huge number of these words are derogatory and disrespectful. Some are simply descriptive, silly, or even quite flowery. I won't bore, amuse, or annoy you with a long list. When the play *The Vagina Monologues* opened in New York City, it was not permitted to be advertised on city buses as most plays were. The word *vagina* was considered too risqué. Author Eve Ensler commented, "What did they want me to call it, *The 'Down There' Monologues?*"

In their book *The Sex You Want: A Lovers' Guide to Women's Sexual Pleasure*, sisters Lisa and Marcia Douglass suggest using the name *cligeva* for the entire female genital crescent. Cligeva cleverly combines *cli*toris, *G*-spot, and *va*gina, with the final "a" also representing the potential pleasure of anal touching. The word covers the whole area quite accurately, although I don't think it has caught on.

TV shows such as *Grey's Anatomy* and *Oprah* have popularized the word *vajayjay*. Maybe you and your partner enjoy pet names for each other's genitals?

Sanskrit words for the sex organs offer dignity and honor. The word for vagina is *yoni*, which means "sacred space." What a wonderful concept—we women have a sacred space within us. In prehistoric times, perhaps before men understood their role in child-making, the womb was honored as a magical place of creation. Ancient temples have been found whose doors represent the vaginal opening: the yoni, a sacred space.

Of course, our sexual pleasure comes not only from *inside* the vagina. The anatomically correct, clinical name for the outer vaginal area is vulva, which includes the clitoris and vaginal lips, or labia. But vulva sounds too much like a car to me.

So my choice for a name is yoni, and I use it to refer to my entire cligeva, clitoris, vulva, vagina, inside and out. On my best days, I feel like I'm all yoni, that my whole body is truly a sacred space. I'll sometimes stretch luxuriously and say to Richard, "I'm all yoni for you," as my skin welcomes his touch. It is also a reminder to him to focus not *only* on my genitals, but to include all of me.

The Sanskrit word for penis is *lingam*, often translated to mean "wand of light." Lingam. Wand of light. Now that's a name! Of course, like yoni, lingam doesn't include the whole "package," all the parts of a man's sexual anatomy. Perhaps there's a word that can enjoyably describe penis, testicles, and prostate, but I haven't come across it yet.

RICHARD SAYS *I like using the words yoni and lingam. They feel honoring, and they come without any baggage attached.*

Using the words lingam and yoni give us a different perspective, an opportunity to honor our bodies, our sexuality, and to help us bring attention to our sex center.

The Sex Squeeze

Energy follows attention. When we place our attention in our sex center, energy follows. A powerful way to bring focus into this part of our body is to actually tighten and release our sex muscles.

This "sex squeeze" is like saying hello to your yoni or lingam and the pubococcygeal (PC) muscles that connect the pubic bone with the coccyx. These are the muscles you would have to squeeze to interrupt a flow of urine.

The subsequent release, the letting go, is even more important than the squeeze. Energy and love flow more freely in Tantra Tai Chi when your sex center is relaxed. In lovemaking, orgasm and bliss can be more fully experienced when your sex center is relaxed.

Not only does it bring your awareness into your body, this little squeeze-and-release exercise is healthy for you, increasing muscle tone, oxygen flow, and circulation. Often called a Kegel, named after the gynecologist who first introduced the practice in the 1940s, this exercise is recommended to new mothers for regaining urinary control after childbirth. Ancient Taoist and Tantra teachings encourage exercising the pelvic floor muscles to increase and prolong sexual pleasure, for both men and women. The perineum, the soft spot behind our genitals, is called the *Hui Yin* point in Chinese medicine. In the Japanese healing system of Reiki, this point is internally tightened as an empowerment of vital energy.

During all the Tantra Tai Chi positions and movements, and during lovemaking, give yourself occasional sex squeezes to keep the sex center alive and to bring your attention into your body.

RICHARD SAYS *The sex squeeze helps me maintain my focus, gets me out of my head, and quiets my mind. I find it very invigorating; it is maybe even my favorite part of Tantra Tai Chi.*

Slower Is Sexier

The slower you do the Tantra Tai Chi movements, the more charge you will create between the two of you. Charge is sexy. Love affairs have charge and intrigue. Adding these qualities to your relationship will definitely give it more zip. Practice Tantra Tai Chi—and lovemaking—slowly, sensually, and deliberately.

Synchronize your Tantra Tai Chi movements with those of your partner. If your partner is moving faster than you, ask him or her to slow down.

In her research for *The Vagina Monologues*, Eve Ensler interviewed hundreds of women. After being asked what their vagina would say if it could speak, the women overwhelmingly, and slowly, said these two words: "Slow down." This is true in Tantra Tai Chi as well as in the bedroom.

RICHARD SAYS *Diana's idea of "slow" is significantly slower than mine—especially in the bedroom.*

Breathing Is Essential

Breathe easily, regularly, in and out. When human beings concentrate and learn new things, we tend to unconsciously hold our breath. So occasionally remind yourself to breathe out. That will start the normal sequence of in and out again, and you won't be holding your breath any more. Allow your breathing to naturally synchronize with each of the Tantra Tai Chi movements. Once you become comfortable with a movement, you can focus even more on your breathing, which will heighten the experience. Conscious breathing increases sensation in the body.

Awakening the Energy

Awakening the Energy is the name of a Tantra Tai Chi movement that effortlessly stimulates your sex center while beginning to create an active bond between you and your partner. It provides a platform for you to acknowledge and share energy together.

In the Awakening the Energy move, you use your hands to slowly make circles in the space between you, as if you are massaging the very molecules of air that join you together. Your hands will be parallel to the ground, palms down, as if they are resting on a tabletop. You will be making slow circles with your hands, keeping the palms down, each hand moving in an opposite direction. Your palms are more sensitive to noticing energy than any other body part. You can feel energy *between* your hands, as you have already practiced in a previous exercise. You might also be able to sense the subtle presence of air that touches your palms during Awakening the Energy. Slow movements are best. When we move slowly, we can be more conscious of what we feel.

Keeping eye contact with your partner, you make slow, continuous circles with your hands, moving them toward your partner and then sweeping them outward and back again to yourself. After nine times, there is a pause, then the direction of the circles is reversed.

When I do this movement with Richard, I feel as if we are both massaging the energy between us. The experience, and sexual awareness, is heightened by holding the sex squeeze for half of each circle and releasing it for the other half. It is especially powerful when we're naked!

After completing Awakening the Energy, when you return to Solo Stillness, you may notice a major difference in how you feel. Have fun and don't worry about doing this or any of the Tantra Tai Chi moves "perfectly." If you and your partner are face-to-face, experimenting with these moves, whatever you do that feels right to you will lead you into greater intimacy.

How to Do Awakening the Energy

❖ Start in Solo Stillness, (see page 48), with your eyes closed. Settle down into your hips. Place your awareness at the bottoms of your feet, as you imagine feeling roots going down into the earth.

❖ Squeeze and release your sex muscles (see page 68). Become connected with yourself.

❈ Open your eyes and wait for your partner's eyes to open. When you have eye contact, step sideways into Connected Pose (see page 55). Say, "I am here" to each other.

❈ Slightly increase the distance between you and your partner by taking a half-step back.

❈ Sink down slightly into your hips, so your knees are relaxed and slightly bent.

❈ While maintaining eye contact, place your hands in front of you, with palms down and fingertips pointed toward your partner.

❈ Move your hands slightly forward toward your partner, then move each hand outward, left hand to the left and right hand to the right, and then circle your hands back to a position in front of you (see Figure 2.4 on the next page).

❈ Hands stay flat, palms down, and relaxed throughout the move.

❈ As you continue to make outward circles with your hands, squeeze and release your sex muscles. You might try tightening the muscles as your hands move forward and releasing the muscles as your hands return toward you.

❈ Make nine circles outward and then pause.

❈ Next, make circles in the opposite direction. Start with your hands in front of you again, fingertips pointed toward your partner. Now move them out to your sides, left hand to the left, right hand to the right, and then toward your partner.

Bring them back toward your sex center and then out to the sides again, circling forward to your partner and back to yourself.

❀ After making nine circles, return to Solo Stillness and close your eyes. Sink into your own hips as you find your feet and sense-feel your roots. Squeeze and release your sex. Relax into your own divine self.

❀ When you feel settled, allow your eyes to open. When your partner's eyes are open, step sideways into Connected Pose.

❀ You can do Awakening the Energy again or you can complete the practice with a namasté bow (see page 62).

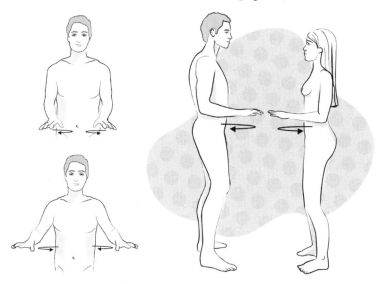

Figure 2.4. Awakening the Energy

The Sex Move

Once you have established a sense of presence and intimacy with your lover through Solo Stillness, the Connected Pose, and Awakening the Energy, you are ready for a movement called the *Sex Move*.

In traditional T'ai Chi programs, the movements have flowery names, often based on the observance of nature: Passing Clouds, Embrace Tiger, Return to Mountain. In Tantra Tai Chi, we keep it simple and to the point. The Sex Move invites you to specifically acknowledge and accept your own sex center, while you are gazing into each other's eyes.

In the Sex Move you'll be rocking your hips and squeezing your sex muscles. Remember to move slowly, breathe, synchronize with one another, and have fun.

How to Do the Sex Move

❖ Start in Solo Stillness (see page 48), with your eyes closed. Settle down into your hips. Place your awareness at the bottoms of your feet as you sense-feel roots going down into the earth.

❖ Squeeze and release your sex muscles (see page 68). Connect with your inner self.

❖ Open your eyes and wait for your partner's eyes to open. When you have eye contact, move one foot to the side into Connected Pose (page 55). Say to each other, "I am here."

❖ Sink down slightly into your hips; let your knees bend.

❈ While maintaining eye contact, synchronize the rocking of your hips and pelvic area toward and away from each other.

❈ As you rock your hips toward your partner, bring your hands forward in front of your sex center, as if you were going to clap. Keep your wrists below your waist and your fingertips pointed downward.

❈ As you rock your hips away from your partner, let your hands also flow backward, to a position behind your hips.

❈ Each time you rock your hips toward your partner, squeeze your sex muscles and bring your hands again in front of you, with fingertips down and palms facing each other, as if you were about to clap.

❈ When you rock your hips away from your partner, release your sex muscles and let your hands flow backward again (see Figure 2.5 on the next page).

❈ Adjust the speed of your forward and backward hip and hand movements to match those of the more slowly moving partner.

❈ Let your breathing harmonize with your movements.

❈ Continue repeating the same forward and backward movement with your hips and hands. Maintain eye contact and feel the energy between you build slightly each time you engage in the movement.

❈ After doing the Sex Move nine times, return to Solo Stillness. Close your eyes and sink into your own hips. Place your

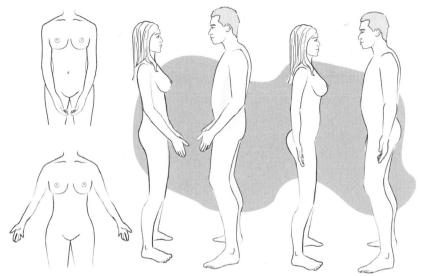

Figure 2.5. The Sex Move

attention in your feet, as you sense-feel your roots going deep into the earth. Squeeze your sex and relax into your own divine self.

❖ When you feel settled, open your eyes. When your partner's eyes are open, step sideways into Connected Pose.

❖ You can repeat the Sex Move, or do another Tantra Tai Chi move, or you can complete the practice with a namasté bow (see page 62).

Three More!
You can enjoy doing any of the Tantra Tai Chi movements for as long as you both like. However, counting can help you maintain

focus. Most Eastern exercises are done in sets of nine, in contrast to Western exercises that use sets of ten or twelve. Nine is considered a sacred number, the number of completion in Eastern philosophy. It is easy to lose count, though. After you have done a move slowly about six times, or whenever one of you is ready to stop, say to the other, "Three more." Then you both do three more of the same movement before returning to Solo Stillness. Saying, "Three more" is a great reminder to be present, to look into each other's eyes as you slowly do those last three moves. Hearing, "Three more" helps you recapture your attention if you have become distracted, as we all are prone to do, by other thoughts.

Like any exercise program you try at home, it can be challenging to practice Tantra Tai Chi without an instructor guiding you, reminding you to breathe, to feel your feet, to bring attention to your sex muscles. You, or your partner, might even feel silly participating on your own in such ritualized movements. Often one person in a couple is more comfortable—or perhaps more motivated—than the other to bring the ceremonial presence of Tantra to your relationship.

Saying ,"Three more" is an easy way for either of you to guide the other without having to be a "teacher." Always be kind and gentle with each other. Any attempt that you make to practice together will add to the depth of your intimate connection.

Richard and I also use the "Three more" signal during our lovemaking sessions. (You'll learn more about this practice in Chapter 3.)

RICHARD SAYS   *It doesn't matter which one of us says, "Three more." It works well for me either way. It enables me to refocus and get back in sync with Diana if my mind has wandered. It makes it easy to end on the same note.*

Oooh-Aaah Variation

Try this variation while doing the Sex Move: Keep eye contact and sensually say, "Oooh" (pronounced *ou* as in "you") when you tighten your sex muscles and rock your hips and hands forward.

Say, "Aaah" as you release the squeeze and tilt your pelvic area backward.

Repeat. Enjoy.

What Next?

The Sex Move builds up energy in the sex center. In everyday lovemaking, sexual energy is usually built up until it is released through genital orgasm. In sacred loving and Tantra practices, this sexual energy is allowed to expand, to move above the waist, into the heart center.

Visualization and intention, along with breath and movement, and squeezing and releasing the genital muscles, are the tools used to move the energy. With these tools, you can stretch the energy upward from its concentration in the sex center until your whole body experiences aliveness. The Heart Move, which you will learn next, encourages and celebrates this flow of energy.

The Heart Center

Some of us know where our heart is—it is the place in the body where we *feel* most things. When we read or hear a moving story, our heart feels touched. We naturally place a hand on our heart in response to startling news. We say things like, "My heart ached for her" or, "I could feel my heart opening again."

We may yearn for our partner to be more in their heart, to be more intimate, to speak about their feelings, dreams, hopes and concerns. But not everyone finds it so easy to be in their heart, to feel what's there. It just isn't their natural habit to experience life from inside the heart; it is not their natural temperament. My husband, Richard, for example, is not a very emotional person. He's a doer: more action-oriented, less emotive, less empathic.

If I keep a green bough in my heart, then the singing bird will come.
CHINESE PROVERB

RICHARD SAYS *I've come a long way. I've learned to appreciate the subtle energies of the heart and the power of those energies when I share them with Diana—especially, but not only, when we are sexual together. Although I will always prefer a game of tennis to an emotionally laden conversation, or any conversation about emotions, I can honestly say I am more aware of my "heart" because of Tantra Tai Chi.*

Modern scientific studies show that directing one's attention to the heart can result in improved health and well-being for the whole body. You can learn to bring attention to this part of the body, even if it is not your nature. When we bring attention to the heart, heart energy and loving feelings automatically arise.

There are actually people who make decisions by tuning into the heart's inner knowing. For example, my friend Bhante Wimala, a Buddhist monk, seems to *think* with his heart. His years of training as a monk make it possible for him to place his entire attention in his heart—instead of his head—to find a solution to whatever problem arises. Standing near him, I can actually feel a shift when he does that. The heart center is a real location in the body. We all have one, just as we all have a sex center, whether or not we are sexually active.

> *When you fish for love, bait with your heart.*
> MARK TWAIN, American author and humorist

In Tantra Tai Chi, the heart center includes not only the physical heart but the whole upper torso area above the waist—the chest, the breasts, even the back. Most of us seem to be divided at the waist. We're either more comfortable and familiar with this area above the waist, the heart center, or with the sex center, below the waist.

I think men relate more easily to their sex center. It is not that they necessarily enjoy sex more than women do or that they masturbate more frequently. Either of these aspects may or may not be true. But men seem to relate more easily to their physical sex center because they have a daily hands-on, ongoing relationship with that part of their body. They hold and aim their penis/-lingam when in the bathroom; they adjust it in their pants. They pay attention to it visually as a barometer of their sexual desire. It is always there, literally in front of them, part of their everyday consciousness.

We women don't have as many reasons to touch or look at our vagina/yoni, outside of experiencing sexual pleasure. Even then, we often use a vibrator. We use toilet paper in the bathroom. And we don't look at other women; we have private stalls. Tampons are usually inserted with an applicator rather than our finger. We're not as hands-on with our sex center in an everyday sense as men are.

However, we women are probably more in touch with the upper part of our body: the chest, the heart center. We adjust our breasts in bras and bathing suits. We examine them monthly for lumps. (Or at least we know we should.) We spread lotion on our faces, neck, and upper torso more often than men do. And, yes, we may be more comfortable with heartfelt emotions than our partners.

Women often grow up with conflicted messages about our sexuality, but we are encouraged to "know our hearts." Many men grow up with emotional constraints on the heart, such as "Big boys don't cry." Men may think that heartfelt dialogue or behavior is unmanly. However when it comes to sex, they usually have less ambiguity.

For some couples, all of this might be reversed. But either way, what's a couple to do if one is more comfortable below the waist and the other is more comfortable above the waist?

As individuals, we can access the power and joy of life available in the heart center without ever venturing below our waist. We can be intimate with others without the charge of sexual energy. And, yes, we can enjoy our sex center, have great sexual experiences, with or without a partner, that have no particular emotional component. Even when it is not about sex itself, we may feel sensations in our genitals when we're excited by a great idea, get a burst of creative energy, or see something breathtakingly beautiful.

When we bring attention to *both* these areas, above and below our waists, we become more centered in the core of our body. We more fully align with our own internal energy flow. And when we share that flow with our most significant other, together, at the same time, magic happens. Then we can really enjoy sex as S.E.X.—**S**ynchronized **E**nergy e**X**change.

Energy Follows Attention

Energy follows attention. Placing our attention in the region of the heart brings energy to our fourth chakra, the heart chakra, and awakens the vibration of love. Like most people who care deeply for their partner, I sometimes feel a surge of love in the area of my heart. You might feel it for your children or for anyone you are fond of. When I notice it, I may say to Richard, "I love you." The words sound outer-directed, but really I'm describing something happening within me. I'm not seeking a reply. It is a great practice for couples to remember to say those words when there is a tangible internal feeling.

When you and your partner purposefully bring attention to your heart centers, you may both experience and more easily express feelings of love.

With attention, the heart center symbolically enlarges to touch the throat area, a channel for the expression of love. At the bottom of the heart center, the solar plexus, with its expanding diaphragmatic breath, helps to more securely anchor the experience in the realm of the body. The solar plexus, heart, and throat are the locations of the third, fourth, and fifth chakras.

Lovemaking can begin first in the heart, and then be moved downward into the lower sex center, or vice versa. Emotional closeness, as well as physical stimulation, can open the doorway into the sexual journey. Tantric lovers learn to stay joined in the heart center even as the sex center awakens into its powerful arousal. Gazing into one another's eyes, couples share the rhythm of life, the music of love.

We can individually find our own sex center by tightening and relaxing those pelvic floor muscles, as in the sex squeeze (see page 68). It is more difficult to internally squeeze our chest area in the same way. Engaging your partner in the following Heart Touching Ceremony will help both of you find your hearts.

The Heart Touching Ceremony

You and your partner can help each other find the heart center with a simple ceremony of touching the heart and saying aloud the word "heart."

Words direct our thoughts and attention. When you say the word "heart" to your partner, your mind will be directed to the experience of awareness in that part of your body that is being touched.

For that moment, you are in your heart. A moment later, you may be distracted by any number of extraneous thoughts. The mind likes to jump around; experienced meditators call this the "monkey mind." However, as soon as you focus yourself in your chest again, and say the word "heart" again, you can return to the immediate experience.

When you add a verbal label to an energy location, it intensifies the consciousness of what you are experiencing. Think of the word "heart" as shorthand for, "I am placing my attention here, in my chest, in my heart center. Will you join me by placing *your* attention in *your* chest, in your heart center? Together, let's synchronize our heart energy."

The Heart Touching Ceremony is a wonderful way to begin experiencing S.E.X.—**S**ynchronized **E**nergy e**X**change. It can be done while sitting, standing, or lying down, as long as you are positioned face-to-face. You can be naked or clothed.

How to Do the Heart Touching Ceremony

❖ Each of you places your right hand on the other's heart center at the middle of the chest.

❖ Using your left hand, adjust your partner's hand on your own body to where it feels best for you, where it feels most comfortable, most aligned with any feeling you may have of your heart center (see Figure 2.6).

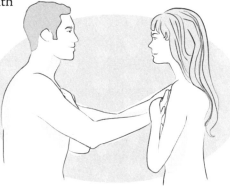

Figure 2.6. Heart Touching Ceremony

❖ Continue to hold one hand on your partner's heart center with your other hand covering your partner's hand, placed on your own heart.

❖ With your eyes open, softly allow your partner to "see" into you. Remember, intimacy means "into-me-see." Sense your beloved seeing into you.

❖ Be aware of both your own breathing and of your partner's breathing as your hands connect your hearts and you gaze into each other's eyes.

❖ Synchronize your breath to create greater intimacy.

❖ When you have brought your attention to your heart center, say the word "heart" aloud to one another.

❖ As you place your attention in the area that is being touched, heart energy, or loving energy, will arise. Again, say the word "heart" aloud.

❖ When you hear your partner say the word "heart," let that be a reminder to feel the hands on your chest, to locate yourself there, in that part of your body, and say the word "heart" back to your partner.

❀ When you feel complete with this practice say, "Three more."

❀ After three more "heart" exchanges, separate and thank each other with a namasté bow (see page 62).

The Heart Move

Now that you both know where the heart center is, you are ready for the Tantra Tai Chi *Heart Move*. In this move, sex and heart support and fuel one another. The movement of energy is ongoing, continuous. There is a back-and-forth flow, a reciprocal circulation of breath, a **S**ynchronized **E**nergy e**X**change.

With practice, the Heart Move can become a very erotic experience, even creating orgasmic shivers along your spine. Because you will be bringing energy up above your waist, be sure to ground yourself afterward with Solo Stillness, connecting with your feet and sense-feeling as if you have roots in the earth.

How to Do the Tantra Tai Chi Heart Move

❀ Begin in Solo Stillness (see page 48), with your eyes closed. Settle down into your hips. Place your awareness at the bottoms of your feet, as you sense-feel roots going down into the earth.

❀ Squeeze and release your sex muscles (see page 68).

❀ Open your eyes and wait for your partner's eyes to open.

When you have eye contact, move one foot to the side into Connected Pose (see page 55).

❊ Sink down slightly farther into your own hips.

❊ Keeping your back upright, sink down slightly more and let your hands come forward as if you're going to do the first part of the Sex Move (see page 74). Maintain eye contact.

❊ Let your body rise a little as your hands carry the energy, weightlessly, all the way up to your heart (see Figure 2.7 on the next page). Keep your shoulders relaxed.

❊ As the hands lift upward, squeeze and hold your sex muscles, and breathe in until your hands reach the heart.

❊ At the heart, turn your hands over, palms downward, and lower them back down.

❊ As the hands lower, sink your body downward slightly, release your breath, and relax the squeeze.

❊ Repeat, raising the hands up to the heart and downward again, in a continuous, sensuous movement.

❊ Sense-feel that energy is coming upward from the earth, through your genitals, up your spine to the heart, and then moving downward again, along with your hands.

❊ Synchronize the speed of the movement with your partner; the faster partner following the pace of the slower partner. Maintain eye contact.

❊ After six moves, or at any time, one of you say to the other, "Three more."

❁ After doing three more Heart Moves, return to Solo Stillness. Bring your feet together, close your eyes, and sense-feel your roots reaching into the ground.

❁ When you feel fully settled, allow your eyes to open. When your partner's eyes are open, step sideways together into Connected Pose.

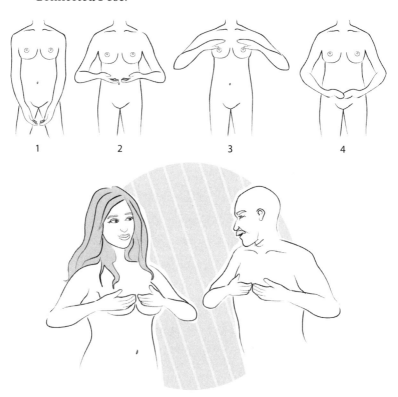

Figure 2.7. The Heart Move

❄ You can do one of the Tantra Tai Chi moves again, or you can complete the practice with a namasté heart salutation (see page 62).

The Heart and Sex Ceremony

When the sex and heart centers are joined, magic happens. It really is that simple. Tantra Tai Chi, along with a ceremonial touch and a spoken word, helps make the joining take place. Words and sounds, flowing from you to your beloved and back again create a dance of energy that will awaken your sexual interest and open your heart. When communicating, it is not always the content of conversation that matters. For some of us, the specific content isn't the primary thing at all. The content can sometimes distract us from the deeper loving presence and conscious attention that we desire.

In the previous Heart Touching Ceremony, you said the word "heart" to each other as you brought attention to the heart center. Now you will be adding the word "sex," as you shift attention to the sex center. In meditation practices, a word, phrase, or sound that is repeated over and over, in order to create focus, is called a *mantra*. The word might have spiritual significance in and of itself, or it may not. In this practice, saying, "Sex" and "Heart" can be considered mantras in that they help you focus. By matching the word with your experience, by bringing attention to the matching part of your body, your whole being participates in the mantra experience.

Remember the childhood song, "I'm a little teapot, short and stout?" You put your hand on your waist to indicate the handle, saying, "Here is my handle," and with your other arm and hand, you mimic the spout, saying, "Here is my spout." In this ceremony, you will use the words "sex" and "heart" in the same way, pointing out to your partner—and reminding yourself—where your attention is being placed. When you say the word "sex," it is as if you were saying, "This is my sex center," as you touch that area. When you say the word "heart," it is as if you were saying, "This is my heart center," as you touch your chest. You are labeling and bringing presence to two different areas of your body.

Only the united beat of sex and heart together can bring ecstasy.
ANAÏS NIN,
The Diary of Anaïs Nin

Richard and I often use this shorthand language, composed of the three words you've learned so far: "sex," "heart," and "eyes." This harmonizes our experience and our presence with one another as we enjoy our **S**ynchronized **E**nergy e**X**change.

The Heart and Sex Ceremony can be done while sitting, standing, or lying down, as long as you are positioned face-to-face. You can be naked or clothed. You can do it for three minutes or for however long it feels comfortable.

How to Do the Heart and Sex Ceremony

❄ Sit facing your partner and maintain eye contact.

❄ Place one hand on your own heart center, located in the middle of your chest, and place the other on your own yoni or lingam, the area of your sex center (see Figure 2.8 on the next page).

- ❁ Say the word "sex" to each other, as you squeeze and release your sex muscles.

- ❁ Say the word "heart" and bring your attention to your chest.

- ❁ You can follow or lead your partner, each of you naming one of these two locations. You may repeat back the same word your partner says or redirect attention to the other location.

- ❁ Maintain eye contact as you engage in a conversation of "sex" and "heart," bringing attention to first one and then the other.

- ❁ Say, "Eyes" if your partner drifts off with eyes closed.

- ❁ If one of you begins to talk about something else, gently bring the dialog back to one of

Figure 2.8. Heart and Sex Ceremony

the three focus words by saying, "Heart," "Sex," or "Eyes."

Variation: Holding Heart and Sex for Your Partner

- ❁ Invite your partner to lie down. Sit by his or her side.

- ❁ Place both your hands on your partner's torso. Let your partner position your hands so one is on the heart center and the other is on the sex center (see Figure 2.9 below). You'll be holding your hands still, not actively massaging or caressing your partner.

❁ Have a "conversation," using only the words "sex," "heart," and "eyes," as you each bring attention to your own and your partner's sex and heart centers.

❁ After five minutes, switch positions so that you are lying down and your partner is sitting by your side with his or her hands on your heart and sex.

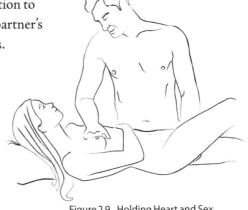

Figure 2.9. Holding Heart and Sex

Sex and Heart: Guiding Your Partner in Self-Loving

In this next ceremonial practice of connecting sex and heart, you will invite your partner to sit by your side and witness you caressing yourself erotically in both areas of your body—your sex center and your heart center. It is possible that you have never touched yourself sexually in front of your partner or, on the other hand, it may be an active part of your love life together. Whether or not this self-pleasuring ceremony is a challenge for you, it is definitely different from conventional masturbation.

You are invited to spend as much time massaging and loving yourself *above* the waist as you do *below* the waist. Consider using oil or lotion on your body and personal lubrication for your more erotic touching. For the pleasuring of a woman, water-based lubricants are often safer than massage oils, which may have additives that irritate the clitoris or the sensitive vaginal walls. Also, although this ceremony does not involve intercourse, if you and your lover choose to use condoms, please be aware that oil can damage the integrity of latex.

There is no goal or requirement of reaching climax or ejaculation, although either may enjoyably occur. And, although sex toys can certainly be fun on other occasions, this ceremonial practice is meant to be *au naturel*, unplugged. You will be giving equal time, consciously and purposefully, to your sex center, your heart center, and the connection between them. Include your whole torso, your breasts, even your face. Caress your belly, your hips, your thighs. Let your touch be tender, loving, sensual, and sexual. Imagine you are doing the Heart Move, tracing the flow upward and downward again, synchronizing it with your breath. Imagine you are showing your partner how you like to be touched and adored. Imagine you are helping your partner become aware of the wholeness of you.

Invite your beloved partner to gaze into your eyes as you touch yourself by saying, "Eyes." Let yourself become aroused. Keep bringing your own attention equally to your sex and to your heart. Indulge yourself but take it easy; don't be in a rush.

There might be times when you want to slow things down, or you just might want to close your eyes for a bit. If this happens, ask for "Solo Stillness." You won't stand up in the Tantra Tai Chi position, but you can close your eyes and rest for a moment within yourself. After awhile, your partner may invite you to open your eyes again by saying, "Eyes."

My personal interest in self-stimulation has varied over the years. There have been times when I felt a compelling urge to pleasure myself daily. There have been periods of no interest at all. This ceremony, massaging and touching myself in a sacred manner, is not dependent on my libido or interest. It is a gift that I can intentionally give to myself and to Richard, regardless of any private activity I may—or may not—also enjoy.

RICHARD SAYS *I was surprised to find that my sexual energy didn't dissipate when I moved attention away from my genitals. Squeezing my sex, and breathing and guiding the energy up to my chest, while keeping eye contact with Diana, really enhances the erotic sensations for me. As I become more comfortable and relaxed with this practice, my sexual energy has gotten stronger and expanded while the sensation of needing to hurry up and ejaculate has lessened. I think it has made me a better lover.*

Be gentle and avoid judging yourself—or your partner—for any feeling of anxiety or embarrassment that either of you may naturally experience.

When you are the witness, maintain eye contact with your partner. You are there to adore, to watch, to be present. The concept of time is very subjective, but if you feel your lover is spending the whole time in sex, or if their hands have stayed totally above the waist for a very long time, your role is to softly guide your partner back to the other area by saying, "Sex" or "Heart." Don't rush them back and forth, but it is your job to encourage or support a balance between the two. Remember, however, that your partner may not need to be guided at all.

While witnessing, you may hold your hands on your own sex and heart. However, I recommend that you neither actively self-pleasure, nor touch your partner. You'll find that sustaining an intimate, nontouching, eyes-open communion with your partner in this way is well worth the challenge.

RICHARD SAYS *It is sometimes difficult for me to focus on Diana's eyes when she is touching her yoni. But the ultimate power of this practice is definitely through the eyes. At other times, however, I do like to watch more closely and learn how she pleasures herself.*

Either of you can say, "Eyes" if your partner's glance strays or if he or she drifts off with closed eyes for more than a few moments. Sometimes it is easier to be in touch with sensual feelings when our eyes are closed, but to create intimacy, you will want to have eye contact.

This can be an amazing experience, as you each raise your sexual energy and then relax it by bringing your attention to the heart. Instead of staying focused on the genitals, you spread the energy upward to your heart and, through your eyes, to your partner.

I suggest that the man be the witness first. After about fifteen minutes, reverse positions and roles. You may wish to embrace one another, with a still, full-body hug. Then sit up and conclude the ceremony with a namasté bow, a heart salutation (see page 62).

The Bindi Center

When the sex and heart centers interact, intimacy will become an irresistible, tangible feeling within you. You may notice your heart opening even more, filled with love for your partner, yourself, your life, and all that surrounds you.

As the two of you continue to blend your sex and heart centers, whether through touch or Tantra Tai Chi movements, an alchemical reaction takes place. You may suddenly notice yourselves experiencing a shift into a spiritual state of mind, an expanded sense of something that is more than sex, more than a personal feeling of love.

Perhaps you already have a name, a label, for this expanded love-space experience from a special time you have shared with your partner—your honeymoon, a particular night of supercharged lovemaking that remains memorable for you both, or your favorite vacation together. Richard and I use the word *bindi* to identify this experience. In Tantra Tai Chi, the bindi center is symbolically located at the upper chakras, the sixth and seventh chakras—the psychic center at the third eye in the forehead and the soul-opening crown chakra at the top of the head. *Bindi* is a Sanskrit word meaning "dot." In a custom derived from Hinduism, bindi dots are used to identify the third eye area. They have even become secular decorations (i.e., nonreligious). (Barbra Streisand wore one in the ending scene in her role as a sex therapist in the movie *Meet the Fockers*.)

Bindi is a derivative of the Sanskrit word *bindu*, meaning "seed," described as the single point of universal creation, the union of male and female, that from which all life springs.

When we connect with bindi, we are connecting not just with our own spiritual center, and not just with our beloved partner, but with all of life. When sex, heart, and bindi are activated and held in alignment, a shift in consciousness is experienced. The sexual energy is transformed from personal to transpersonal, from separateness to oneness. Entering the bindi space indicates a move away from ego, personality, anything that defines or divides. This experience cannot be forced or demanded. It simply appears when we are present for it.

Light in the Head

The bindi center is related to light, which is important for our health. For example, the pineal gland, located in the center of the brain, in the bindi center, controls the production of melatonin and is responsible for how we react to sunlight. There's a condition called seasonal affective disorder, or SAD, that can occur when we don't get enough sunlight and the pineal gland is not functioning at an optimum level. (If you feel you may have SAD, I recommend Fiona Marshall and Peter Cheever's book on the subject, *Positive Options for Seasonal Affective Disorder*.)

Dedicated meditators sometimes report a fountain of light gushing out the top of their heads, or surrounding their heads like a halo. In the T'ai Chi Chih program that Richard and I teach, there is a move called Light at the Top of the Head.

When we first began experiencing the blend of sex and heart, and the subsequent shift that occurred, it felt like a point of light or a lightbulb going off in our heads. The word *enlightenment* came to mind, and in honor of all this light, and our spiritual potential, Richard and I chose to name this upper Tantra Tai Chi center *bindi*. (At one of our Intimacy Retreats, the couples renamed it "bingo!")

Bindi describes those moments in lovemaking when time stops—those moments when you look at your partner in full awareness of the love you share. When you identify and acknowledge bindi at the same time as your lover does, your shared enjoyment of sex truly becomes a Synchronized Energy eXchange.

So far, you have learned to place your awareness in the sex center by consciously exercising your sex muscles. Your partner's hand on your heart center helped you locate that part of your body. A touch or massage from your partner on *any* body part can be a delightful way of focusing attention. Tapping on your partner's forehead as orgasmic energy is building can expand your partner's focus from the sex, through the heart, to the bindi.

A ceremonial way to honor the bindi center is to apply a bindi dot. Stick-on dots are available at Indian boutiques or on-line and even in some cosmetics or fashion stores. You can use nontoxic paste, glitter glue, or a washable felt marker to apply a homemade decorative dot to one another's foreheads, or paint one on with lipstick or a dash of henna.

RICHARD SAYS *I love seeing a bindi dot on Diana. It reminds me of our connection and turns me on.*

How to Do the Bindi Dot Ceremony

❁ While sitting or standing in front of your partner, apply a bindi dot (or perhaps a ceremonial kiss) to your partner's forehead, centered above and between the eyebrows (see Figure 2.10).

❁ Tell your partner that you honor his or her spiritual essence. Use her or his name. Say whatever feels meaningful to you.

❁ End the ceremony with a namasté bow (see page 62).

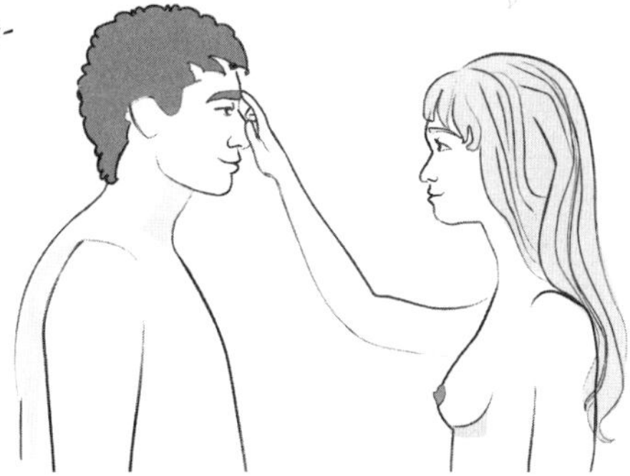

Figure 2.10. Bindi Dot Ceremony

The Bindi Move

Bindi, although symbolized by the dot at the forehead or an energy center in the middle of the brain, is more of an experience than a physical location. The awakened mind is not specifically situated in the head.

The *Bindi Move* in Tantra Tai Chi honors and acknowledges this subtle—and sometimes not so subtle—shift into a *sattvic*, tantric level of blissful and ecstatic love.

The conscious direction of energy and attention between the sex center and the heart center is the basic activity of Tantra Tai Chi. As these centers are stimulated, you enliven a sense of the spiritual, a sensation of universal wholeness.

The Bindi Move begins similarly to the Heart Move. However, instead of only coming up to the chest level, the hands are brought all the way up to the forehead, to the third eye area, and then opened outward to encompass the space, the aura, around you and your beloved partner.

As in all the Tantra Tai Chi moves, do it slowly, synchronizing with your partner, with eyes open and with a spirit of love.

How to Do the Tantra Tai Chi Bindi Move

❖ Begin in Solo Stillness (see page 48), with your eyes closed. Place your awareness at the bottoms of your feet as you sense-feel roots going down into the earth.

❖ Squeeze and release your sex muscles (see page 68).

❊ Open your eyes. When you have eye contact with your partner, step sideways together into Connected Pose (see page 55).

❊ Start as if you are beginning the Heart Move (see page 86), but let your hands rise all the way up to your forehead. Keep your shoulders relaxed.

❊ As the hands lift upward, squeeze and hold your sex muscles and breathe in until your hands are at or above your forehead.

❊ At the forehead, turn your hands palm outward and let each describe a large circle outward and back downward to the earth and your sex center (see Figure 2.11 on page 102).

❊ As the hands lower, sink downward slightly, release your breath, and relax the squeeze.

❊ Repeat the exercise, raising the hands upward above the forehead and outward again, in a continuous, sensuous movement.

❊ Sense-feel that energy is coming up from the earth, through your genitals, up your spine to the top of your head, and then releasing outward.

❊ Synchronize the movement with your partner, by following the pace set by the slower partner. Maintain eye contact.

❊ After six moves, or at any time, one of you can say to the other, "Three more."

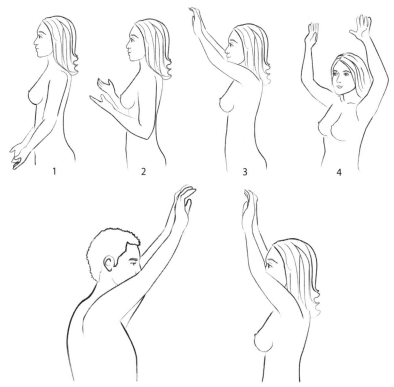

Figure 2.11. The Bindi Move

❈ After doing three more Bindi Moves, return to Solo Stillness, bring your feet together, and close your eyes. Sense-feel your roots reaching into the ground.

❈ When you feel fully settled, open your eyes. When your partner's eyes are open, step sideways together into Connected Pose.

❄ Do another Tantra Tai Chi move or complete the practice with a namasté heart salutation (see page 62).

The Tantra Tai Chi Trilogy

The *Tantra Tai Chi Trilogy* is a combination of three moves you have already learned, with the added emphasis of naming each of the centers—sex, heart, and bindi. You and your partner will do a Sex Move, saying, "Sex." Then you do a Heart Move, saying, "Heart." Next is a Bindi Move, as you say, "Bindi!" Synchronizing your moves together, you return to the Sex Move, again saying, "Sex." Then you continue to repeat the entire pattern.

Combining the moves in this way anchors your language with the center you are naming. Richard and I use this three-word ceremonial language whenever we want to have S.E.X.—Synchronized Energy eXchange—even during lovemaking itself. The verbal trilogy defines and shapes our shared experience of love. The words remind us of the Tantra Tai Chi moves and resonate within our bodies.

Although I cannot know exactly what Richard is experiencing when he looks at me and says, "Heart," I do know that his voice sounds different when he says, "Sex," so his experience must be different. It is not likely that we are both having exactly the same experience, but when I look into his eyes, and say, "Heart" back to him, bringing my attention to that place in my body, we become joined in a most magical way. When we both say, "Bindi!" it feels to me as if the universe opens and welcomes us into itself. I can never know for sure what Richard is actually experiencing, but together we can journey into the joyful here-and-now of our sacred embrace.

When appropriate, in both Tantra Tai Chi and during love-making, we ask for the other's "eyes," and we often affirm our presence with each other by saying, "I am here."

RICHARD SAYS *Sometimes I say, "Sex" or "Heart" to Diana, even in a regular conversation. It helps remind both of us that we're lovers with a special connection.*

How to Do the Tantra Tai Chi Trilogy

❖ Begin in Solo Stillness (page 48), with your eyes closed. Place your awareness at the bottoms of your feet as you sense-feel roots going down into the earth.

❖ Squeeze and release your sex muscles (see page 68).

❖ Open your eyes. When you have eye contact with your partner, step sideways together into Connected Pose (see page 55).

❖ Together, do a Sex Move (see page 74) and say, "Sex," as your hands are in front of your sex center (see Figure 2.12 on the next page).

❖ Then do a Heart Move (see page 86) and say, "Heart," as your hands are in front of your heart center (see Figure 2.12 on the next page).

❖ Then, do a Bindi Move (see page 100) and say, "Bindi!" as your hands reach the forehead and open outward, celebrating the bindi center (see Figure 2.12 on the next page).

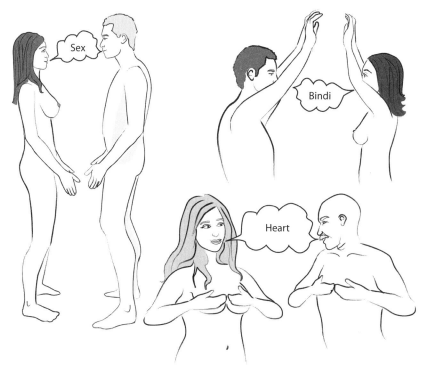

Figure 2.12. The Tantra Tai Chi Trilogy

❖ Repeat the sequence as often as you like, each time saying the words aloud at each center.

❖ To end the exercise, bring your feet together and give each other the ceremonial namasté bow (see page 62).

When Richard and I engage in the Tantra Tai Chi exercises together, we celebrate and deepen our passion for one another. Tantric sex takes our passion to another level.

3

Tantric Sex

Tantric sex is physical intimacy that fulfills the larger purpose of spiritual union. Tantric sex can be any sexual engagement that links you intimately with your beloved and joins you in a blended dance of sexual, emotional, and spiritual wholeness.

You can enjoy tantric sex as a formal, ceremonial ritual or as a brief, casual interlude in the midst of more robust sexual activity. In Tantra, everything is sacred—both the physical and the spiritual—so be sure not to judge your partner for his or her preferred way of manifesting sexual energy.

Experiment, explore, and discover what evokes a shared experience of infinite love for the two of you. There is no right or wrong way to experience bliss. You can spend hours together, if and when you have the time and inclination, or you can rekindle your passion daily, as Richard and I do, with a ten-minute intimate practice.

The Tantra Tai Chi Trilogy
in the Bedroom

Some people say that the afterglow, that deep contentment of resting in one another's arms, is the best part of sex.

in the afterglow
the world
my world
seems softer
somehow
less intense
and pressing

in the afterglow
the demands
my demands
appear less worthy
somehow
of so much frivolous
attention

in the afterglow
the concerns
my concerns
melt away
somehow
leaving my heart
open and ready
to embrace
everything

This is just how I feel during my daily ten minutes of tantric sex with Richard. It is as if everything else melts away, leaving us open and ready to embrace not only each other but also the whole universe. It is a meditation, a time of timelessness. Yet it is also sexual. Tantra Tai Chi teaches you how to bring your attention inside your body, aligning you with your lover and also with your own core energy. During tantric sex, using the same trilogy of sex, heart, and bindi you can create a dynamic shift into this longed-for state of intimate union. You can transform sexual activity from an active, goal-oriented release of genital tension (climax/ejaculation) into the slower, sacred journey of full-body, blissful, orgasmic expansion that Richard and I call Peaceful Passion.

It is good to have an end to journey toward, but it is the journey that matters, in the end.
URSULA LE GUIN,
American author

Peaceful Passion

Peaceful Passion—that sounds like two different things, doesn't it? Passion is hot, sexy, and full of fire. Peace is soft and graceful. Peaceful Passion is a sacred and ceremonial union of opposites, an intentional lovemaking that blends body, heart, and spirit into an experience of infinite delight. Peaceful Passion allows you to enjoy sexual connection in an easy, effortless, incredibly rewarding way, regardless of your age or sexual appetite.

Peaceful Passion is a unique solution to the age-old impasse between sex and heart that keeps so many couples from enjoying the intimacy they crave. Setting the intention of your lovemaking to be Peaceful Passion, you and your beloved can enter into *sattvic*, sacred, tantric sexuality.

You may be thinking, "What?" Isn't lovemaking supposed to be filled with vigorous activity, stimulation, erotic tension, and release? Isn't the purpose of sex to achieve that release, reach a climax, have an ejaculation? Aren't bigger, better, and more numerous orgasms the goal? Well, first of all, there are no "supposed-to-be's" in healthy sexuality. And yes, active, aerobic, *rajasic* sex play can be wonderful!

Tantric sex, however, in its highest evolution, involves a purposeful sharing of physical love and spiritual connection that can, but does not always, end in climax or ejaculation. It is an unconventional approach to lovemaking that is truly about creating love.

Peaceful Passion, without the pumping, the grinding, the climax, or the ejaculation, takes us directly into our hearts, reliably awakening our love for one another in the context of an even greater, abiding orgasm. In Peaceful Passion, you remain relaxed, conscious, and aware. Your bodies, minds, and souls are at rest.

Physical satisfaction alone doesn't always satisfy the heart's longing for intimate connection. Peaceful Passion provides the conscious realization of our union with universal oneness.

In Peaceful Passion, sexual union is enjoyed for the purpose of creating and celebrating love, intimacy, closeness, and a sense of belonging. Remember, intimacy means "into-me-see." Peaceful Passion offers an experience of being acknowledged, being present, and being seen, one soul to another.

And while providing the calming benefits of meditation and a connection with love and spirit, Peaceful Passion also gives a delicious and juicy charge to your sexual batteries. Most importantly, especially if you're short on time or energy, this can really all happen in only ten minutes! Richard and I love our ten minutes of Peaceful Passion, every day. I hope you can fit something like this into your schedule, too.

RICHARD SAYS *I always look forward to our daily practice of Peaceful Passion. It is sensual and energizing and a marvelous way to keep our relationship alive and fun.*

What to Do During Peaceful Passion

During Peaceful Passion, you apply the principles of Tantra Tai Chi. You become present with each other in each of those centers, as you share aloud an open-eyed dialog consisting of the words "sex," "heart," and "bindi."

You relax into the incredible flow of love as it arises. You won't be on a mission to reach, or help each other reach, climax or ejaculation. Instead, reminding and guiding each other, you establish a rhythm of acknowledging those three centers, visiting each one together. As in the Tantra Tai Chi Trilogy, together you bring your attention to your sex centers, and say, "Sex," and then switch the attention to your heart centers, saying, "Heart."

You will soon move beyond your personal boundaries into the welcoming delight of bindi.

Experiment in creating the best way for Peaceful Passion to work for you. Always be kind and gentle with each other in the sacred space of Peaceful Passion. Let the energy of your genitals and heart awaken the bindi. Enjoy the closeness and let the experience unfold. Squeeze and release your sex muscles and say, "Sex" to each other. Sense a flow of energy reaching up to your hearts. Breathe into your hearts, touch each other's hearts and say, "Heart." Say, "I am here" to each other. Recognize bindi through your eyes.

You can also invite one another to bring attention to any other body parts—elbows, hips, knees, toes. Right now, while reading this book, take a moment to be aware of your right thumb. Sense-feel the whole of your right thumb. Place your attention right there, in your right thumb. Now shift your attention to your left thumb. When you feel this shift take place, you are experiencing body awareness. Synchronizing your presence with your partner through body awareness is the secret to experiencing sex as a Synchronized Energy eXchange.

When you harmonize with each other's energy through Peaceful Passion, you join sexually with your beloved at a soul level. You create balance, alignment, and vitality in your relationship, and in your life. With consistent practice over time, the urgency to ejaculate, the desire for climax, is eventually replaced by the quiet, orgasmic joy of shared intimacy. And you can still enjoy lusty sexual sessions at other times. Peaceful Passion is a nutritious rendezvous that can enhance your relationship every day. Passion is stimulated by the tension of separating and coming back together, as in the Tantra Tai Chi positions of Solo Stillness and Connected Pose. During lovemaking, you do not stand up in the actual positions. You can create the same energetic pulsation by pausing, closing your eyes to connect with your inner self, and then reconnecting with each other with your eyes open. This occasional pause, and the act of switching back and forth between eyes closed and eyes open, will move you and your partner into deeper and deeper levels of intimacy, taking you beyond yourselves into the spiritual realms of unconditional ecstasy.

Like many women, I experience climax most easily with clitoral and/or G-spot stimulation, both of which receive a lot of attention in the Yin Massage (see page 145). So it seems odd for me to recommend intercourse positions that do not specifically hit either of those sensitive areas. Peaceful Passion is not traditional intercourse. The lingam/penis is placed inside the yoni/vagina, but there is no active thrusting. Your entire focus during the experience is on the Tantra Tai Chi pattern of sex, heart, and bindi.

Of course, intercourse is not the only item on the sexual menu that you and your partner might share or desire. Kissing of lips and breasts, oral sex, genital massage, and many other activities are delightful erotic play and no menu would be complete without them. Peaceful Passion is a meaningful, sexual intercourse ceremony of love and intimacy that propels you into the awesome beauty of the present moment. It is simply amazing, and easy to do on a daily basis.

No Foreplay. No Erection.

One thing that's great about Peaceful Passion is that it can be entered into without any stimulation, without foreplay, and even without an erection.

Although I realize that an entire industry exists to help men have better erections, a stiff member is not required for Peaceful Passion. Richard tells me that he used to focus most of his sexual energy on maintaining an erection. And I used to think that if he didn't have an erection, he wasn't interested in sex with me. That was before we began thinking of sex as a **S**ynchronized **En**ergy e**X**change, a shared and loving meditation.

Not only can you enjoy Peaceful Passion if the man has a soft or semi-erect lingam, it is sometimes easier that way! And while pleasuring of the female partner is lovely and helps to prepare the yoni, a personal lubricant product can ease the way quite nicely. Personal lubricants have become more available than ever. What this means is that you can get together for Peaceful Passion *by appointment*, without having to be in the mood. Neither of you has to feel "ready" or even energetic. Note, however, that lubricant is not a form of birth control, nor does it prevent the transmission of infections. Also, watch out for additives in lubrications that might cause an irritation. Have fun experimenting until you find the one that works best for you.

Some sacred sexuality teachings state that a couple must remain in this type of sexual embrace for at least an hour in order to reap the deeper benefits of sacred union. However, using the principles of Tantra Tai Chi, you can enter much more quickly into the experience of **S**ynchronized **E**nergy e**X**change, sometimes instantaneously. Ten minutes of Peaceful Passion can be thought of as a sacred "quickie." Sometimes you will want to spend more time, but ten minutes a day is a do-able commitment.

Once you have experienced the high feelings of Peaceful Passion, you'll always want to show up for your agreed-upon appointment time, even if you're not feeling well. Headache excuses or "I'm too tired" will become a thing of the past.

Orgasm and Ejaculation: What's the Difference?

Ejaculation and orgasm are two separate events. Ejaculation is a feel-good physical release of fluid. Orgasm can be used to describe the mental/emotional/spiritual experience of expansion that accompanies sexual release. Although ejaculation and orgasm generally occur together, one can happen without the other. Typically, when a man ejaculates and orgasms, the lovemaking ends. When tantric sex takes place without ejaculation, energy is moved from the genitals up to the heart and beyond. The experience of orgasm and intimate love can therefore be prolonged or be revisited over and over again without ending the lovemaking experience. (Why do they call ejaculation "coming," when we know it means he's "leaving"?)

Some Taoist and Tantra traditions suggest that the woman be encouraged to climax, even multiple times, but that the man withhold from ejaculating. Others promote a style of lovemaking in which *neither* the man nor the woman "comes."

Personally, I love the experience of climaxing, and Richard also certainly loves to ejaculate. I'm not suggesting these sensations be eliminated, and in the next chapter I encourage you to enjoy the Yin and Yang Massages, which provide lots of opportunity for both.

However, our favorite tantric sexual practice on a daily basis is always Peaceful Passion, during which, surprisingly, neither of us has a conventional orgasm—one involving either climax or ejaculation.

RICHARD SAYS *I like conventional orgasms with ejaculation as much as anyone, but the tantric approach enables me to walk around all day sexually charged and in love. That's a good feeling and very positive for our relationship. I prefer it to three seconds of blissful ejaculation.*

Nonejaculatory Intercourse: Influencing the Hormones of Love

Ancient teachings, as well as modern theories, explain and promote the benefits of nonejaculatory intercourse. It was once thought that a man's life force—his spirit, or "*jing*"—was contained in his semen and that he would live longer if he ejaculated less. Although longevity is not assured by retaining semen, and may not even contribute to it at all, Richard tells me that his ongoing energy level has increased tremendously since practicing the Peaceful Passion style of lovemaking.

The experience of sexual intimacy without climax or ejaculation may also produce and be influenced by a variety of biochemical substances and hormones in our bodies. Oxytocin, for example, strengthens the feeling of being emotionally bonded. My heart floods open during tantric lovemaking with Richard; it is as if I can feel the oxytocin directing me to love him with all of my heart. Oxytocin may trigger the production of endorphins, which are responsible for the "high" feeling associated with pleasurable activities.

Dopamine, a chemical in the brain, is said to increase sex drive. There is definitely a sexual charge as you return over and over again to the Tantra Tai Chi pattern of bringing attention to your sex center, helped by the squeezing and releasing of the sex muscles. Ejaculation and climax can result in a blowout burst of dopamine, similar to the temporary charge delivered by caffeine, drugs, high-energy sports, and other potentially addictive activities. Yet this enjoyable explosion is often followed by a major drop-off of energy, an abrupt disconnection on the part of each partner as we fall asleep or reach for the TV remote.

Research now suggests that this immediate turnaway from the person who just moments ago was the center of our universe might actually be caused by that fun burst of dopamine (for a studied analysis of nonejaculatory intercourse, see *Cupid's Poisoned Arrow: From Habit to Harmony in Sexual Relationships* by Marnia Robinson). With the dopamine gone, there can be an upsurge of prolactin, a hormone that actually shuts off our sexual interest. Produced also during breast-feeding, prolactin keeps us from being sexually interested in the person we are with.

Although women can often climax without losing sexual energy and continue to be ready for more stimulation and yet another climax, sometimes we too lose interest in our partner after the burst itself. A more sustained level of dopamine may be maintained by making love without climax or ejaculation. Passion stays alive in a relationship when our sexual interest is kept alive.

During tantric sex, sexual energy does not fall off. It is continuously cycled through the heart and bindi centers. Instead of focusing all that energy just in the genitals, where it would tend to explode, we consciously and intentionally allow it to expand throughout our whole body.

Serotonin, another brain chemical, is valued for its antidepressant qualities and is thought to be increased during meditation. In tantric sex, a meditative tranquility is noticeable as soon as the bindi center comes alive. A feeling of extreme well-being fills both partners. Richard and I acknowledge this shift in consciousness by saying, "Bindi" to each other, and we abide there for awhile, usually with huge loving smiles breaking out upon our faces. Then we return our attention to the sex center by squeezing and releasing our sex muscles and saying, "Sex." Back and forth we go, guiding each other between sex and heart, always being open to those delicious, soul-warming, afterglow sensations of bindi.

Encouraged and elicited by the pattern of sex/heart/bindi, both the excitement of sexual arousal and a state of peaceful love can be enjoyed at the same time. The positive effects of dopamine, oxytocin, and serotonin are all available while enjoying tantric sex.

It is not so much an issue of learning to control or prevent ejaculation. The opening and relaxing of the whole self takes pressure off the groin area and allows the energy to move in an ever-widening pathway. Unmistakable, palpable experiences of joyful, loving orgasm are simply allowed to take place without any accompanying ejaculation or climax.

RICHARD SAYS   *The Tantra Tai Chi exercises have taught me how to stay relaxed and yet sexually focused. It is not really about preventing an ejaculation. It is more about allowing myself to be in love with Diana and letting our sexual energy blend. The verbal part of the exercises, saying, "Sex" and "Heart," and bringing my attention to those areas, really helps.*

The wisdom of Tantra tells us that we can only learn through our own experience, so you will have to try these lovemaking ideas yourself to understand how fabulous they can be.

RICHARD SAYS   *Once Diana and I brought Tantra Tai Chi into the bedroom on a daily basis, our whole universe*

*shifted. Sex became a part of—and remains—at the top of
our daily agenda, no longer a hit-or-miss event dependent on
the timing of our individual sex drives.*

Best Positions for Peaceful Passion

Although any sexual activity or position can be used for the
Peaceful Passion approach to tantric sex, the principles are applied most easily when you are comfortably positioned face-to-
face with your beloved.

Yab Yum

A seated Peaceful Passion position, called *Yab Yum* (meaning
"Father-Mother" in Sanskrit), emphasizes the male/female balance, and it highlights the union of the two. In classical Tantra
teachings this sitting position is part of a sexual ritual called *maithuna*.

If you are already engaged in intercourse, you can pause to
reposition or roll yourselves up into this sitting position. Once
there, begin to guide each other through a subtle version of the
Tantra Tai Chi moves, by calling attention to your sex and heart
centers, and celebrating bindi.

Your focus will slow down from a thrusting rhythm—which
is difficult in this position—to a more intimate sex/heart/bindi
appreciation. Yab Yum provides an excellent opportunity to explore the sensually connected potential of Tantra Tai Chi.

Name each location, and imagine that you're doing the Tantra Tai Chi Trilogy. By speaking the words aloud, you align both

your physical and mental attention on your body, limiting the potential distraction caused by all the other thoughts that your mind is constantly producing. Emotional presence follows, preparing the way for spiritual bliss, all within a sexual framework.

To experience Yab Yum, the woman sits on her partner's lap with her legs wrapped around him, sometimes touching the soles of her feet together (see Figure 3.1). A pillow can be placed underneath her to provide more comfort. His legs may be crossed in Indian style, stretched straight out, or even placed over the side of the bed.

Figure 3.1. Yab Yum

You can sit in Yab Yum with or without sexual penetration. If your partner invites you to sit on his lap, and he already has an erection, you may not be ready—or interested—in hopping on! But that doesn't mean you have to say no to a loving time together. Instead, you can sit on his lap with the erect lingam between you. Snuggle up against him as you synchronize your energy centers—and your anatomy. It is usually helpful to apply some personal lubricant to provide comfort and added pleasure.

In the same way, if the man does not have an erection, the woman can sit on his lap with his relaxed lingam resting against her yoni.

RICHARD SAYS *Putting pressure on Diana's clitoris with my lingam always brings a smile to her face.*

Either of you can invite the other to sit in Yab Yum. No one has to be "ready," or desirous for sex, and no one has to "perform." The whole concept of performance in sex is often an obstacle to the enjoyment and sharing of love.

If you do begin with penetration, rolling up into the sitting position from either missionary or woman-on-top, the man's erection may lessen or even disappear while you sit in Yab Yum. This happened to Richard, which led to the amazing discovery that his sexual energy could flow with or without an erection.

When Richard and I first started experimenting with Yab Yum, we had not yet developed the Tantra Tai Chi pattern of sex/heart/bindi focus. We would sit quietly for a short while, gazing into each other's eyes, but I suspect our thoughts were sometimes miles apart. I could be silently absorbed in a meditative heart space, while Richard might have been noticing—and becoming concerned—that his erection was diminishing. Suddenly, he would return us to a position where he could more comfortably thrust and regain penile hardness.

RICHARD SAYS   *When I first tried sitting in the Yab Yum position, which doesn't allow for much thrusting, I didn't maintain it for very long. Not wanting to lose my erection, I would maneuver us back into a more familiar, more active, position. Now that I have the Tantra Tai Chi Trilogy—I think of it as a skill set—I am more focused on the joy of sexual energy itself, and this position has become one of my favorites.*

In addition to applying the pattern from Tantra Tai Chi, you can create your own ritual or ceremony to use during Yab Yum. For example, if you know a breathing or chanting practice that you have learned elsewhere, you can share it during Yab Yum with your partner. You can even sing or recite poetry to each other! The important thing is to keep each other engaged in being present.

It really helps to remind each other of the sex and heart centers, with simple verbal acknowledgments. Squeeze and release your sex muscles, inviting each other to be in the sex center. Say, "Sex." Breathe in and out of the heart, and remind each other to be in the heart center. Say, "Heart." The words keep your attention focused on your physical presence with each other.

Bindi, the spiritual opening, often feels like grace, magically appearing as a transformational moment of transcendent love. When you feel this spiritual opening, be sure to say, "Bindi," or whatever word describes that experience for you both.

It took time for Richard and me to fully appreciate that sexual union does not have to have orgasmic explosion as a goal or an ending. With an understanding of the Tantra Tai Chi principles, it is now easier for us—and now, you!—to enjoy this type of lovemaking.

Open Yab Yum

"Open Yab Yum" is our name for another, more relaxed sitting position. Called the "posture of the future" by Dr. Paul Pearsall in his classic study of marital sex entitled *Super Marital Sex*, it allows for more comfortable back support for both people. Both of you can lean on pillows against a wall or headboard, a stack of floor pillows, or Backjack chairs. When you sit in Open Yab Yum, the man does not have to hold his partner's weight on his legs. To try this position, sit so that your genitals are very close or touching (see Figure 3.2). You can use your hands to explore one another's sex and heart centers. An erection is not necessary. All that is required is that each of you is willing to enter into the presence of your love.

Open Yab Yum provides room for sensual touching and

Figure 3.2. Open Yab Yum

stimulation of one another's bodies. The lingam, whether hard or soft, feels good when held against the clitoris, and the pressure on the clitoris provides an additional charge. You will be surprised at the number of orgasms—or "lovegasms"—you can generate, even in this relaxed position.

Be sure to continue the Tantra Tai Chi dialogue with each other as you say and experience, "Sex," "Heart," and "Bindi." You might even like to sit in this position to talk about whatever else needs discussing. What model car to buy? Where to take your next vacation? Richard and I have had many of our business meetings sitting in the Open Yab Yum position!

RICHARD SAYS *The open yab yum position really worked for us during a time when I was going through a downturn in my sexual drive. It was the forerunner to our current daily practice of Peaceful Passion.*

Sideways Yab Yum

Richard and I particularly love this sideways version of Yab Yum. It is without a doubt our favorite way to enjoy Peaceful Passion on a daily basis. Lying sideways together is easier on Richard's legs than the traditional Yab Yum sitting position. Keeping my knee high up under his waist prevents pressure on my leg, as long as we're not on a hard surface.

If you are already engaged in intercourse, you can simply wrap around each other in this sideways hug (see Figure 3.3 on the next page) and begin focusing on sex, heart, and bindi.

Figure 3.3. Peaceful Passion: Sideways Yab Yum

Or, you might like to start the way Richard and I do for our ten-minute daily practice. Begin by sitting facing your best directions (see page 40). Take a moment to gaze into one another's eyes. Breathe together. Smile! Acknowledge out loud that you are here to share love. Expressing love and appreciation for one another both before and after Peaceful Passion will add to the strengthening of your relationship.

To enter into Peaceful Passion without an erection and without foreplay, Richard and I move into a scissors position, which makes penetration possible, even with a soft lingam.

RICHARD SAYS   *During one of my early prostate massages (see page 170), I experienced total orgasmic joy without having an erection. That blew my mind and has allowed me to give up my attachment to thinking about my erection during lovemaking. Instead, I can now give more attention and love to Diana.*

To permit entry of a soft lingam into the yoni, the woman reclines on her back, looking at her partner, while he lies next to her, on his side, facing her. (Richard and I find it most comfortable for him to lie to the right of me.)

With the man lying to her right, the woman lifts her right leg and places it on top of both of his legs. The man places both his legs around her left leg, which is the one farthest away from him. His right leg is now between her two legs. Both people then adjust so that their genital areas are brought close together (see Figure 3.4 below). Experiment to find the best way to allow the lingam to nestle against the yoni. You might find yourselves at right angles to each other. You may need to raise her hips with pillows or find a different position that works better for you. With practice, the fit will come naturally.

Once the genitals are close together, anoint his lingam and her yoni with lubricant. Do not use too much lubricant, but

Figure 3.4. Soft entry for Peaceful Passion: scissors position

rather just enough to create a slippery surface. The woman can take his lingam gently into her hands. She can playfully introduce the lingam to her yoni, with some caressing of her vaginal lips and clitoris. Then, she actually "stuffs" the lingam, or at least the head, into her yoni. As she relaxes and opens, the lingam is drawn farther into her. The lingam may—or may not—become more erect, as the yoni continues to relax and open.

If the lingam is temporarily too large to be comfortably eased into a not-yet-awakened yoni, you might try talking about something else for a short time, distracting his excitement. Generally, erections reduce without attention, unless an erectile enhancing drug has been taken.

Richard has told me of methods he learned while serving as an Army medic, methods used to reduce erections in his patients, such as flicking the head of the penis with a spoon, but I've never tried any of these methods. An alternative—and fun—solution is for us to awaken my yoni more—although this might lead us to a sexual engagement with more action than Peaceful Passion! In a healthy relationship, all mutually desired sexual activity is certainly acceptable.

In the Peaceful Passion soft-lingam approach, the first moment of entry may or may not be remarkable. The lingam and yoni love to be together, but they are more familiar with friction than with stillness. It takes time for them both to become sensitive to the subtle surge of love that this connection brings about.

RICHARD SAYS *When I join with Diana in Peaceful Passion, there is an immediate rush of energy from my lingam to my heart, which I would never have thought possible. This loving connection is my daily vitamin.*

Actually, Richard and I do not remain in the scissors position for very long. In a sex-advice column, I once saw the scissors position recommended for early morning sex, before you and your partner have had a chance to brush your teeth. It was called the "dragon breath" position! But for us, it feels more intimate if our faces are closer together. Also, if I remain on my back with my head turned toward him, I will soon get a stiff neck.

In order for the woman to turn more directly toward her partner, she can bring both of her legs onto the top of his legs. She can then shift her body so that she is on her side instead of on her back, while still keeping the genitals together (see Figure 3.5 below). She can use the sex squeeze to hold him in, although sometimes too much squeeze can push him out. Remember to

Figure 3.5. Soft entry for Peaceful Passion: legs-over position

keep humor available! This legs-over position can be very relaxing, and it is a good place to check in with each other, at your sex, heart, and bindi centers.

From here, Richard and I continue into our personal favorite Peaceful Passion position, so that we can be not only face-to-face but also completely body-to-body. The woman lifts her right leg completely over his head to make room for him to move on top of her momentarily, missionary style (see Figures 3.6 and 3.7 below). It sounds amazing, but all of this can be accomplished without an erection.

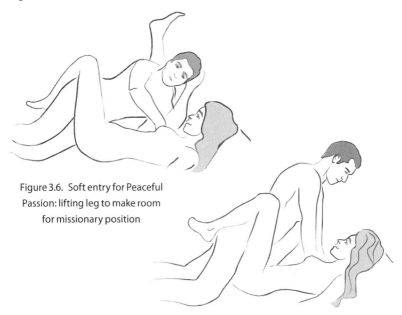

Figure 3.6. Soft entry for Peaceful Passion: lifting leg to make room for missionary position

Figure 3.7. Soft entry for Peaceful Passion: missionary position

She then wraps her legs around his waist as they lay again on their sides, together, in the sideways Yab Yum position (see Figures 3.8 and 3.9 below). Once in this position, share aloud the Tantra Tai Chi Trilogy pattern of "sex," "heart," and "bindi." Say the words aloud, bring your attention to each center, and enjoy the bliss.

Have lots of pillows handy to assure your comfort, because you will want to stay in this position for at least ten minutes, if that is your commitment, or perhaps for even much longer.

Figure 3.8. Soft entry for Peaceful Passion: wrapping legs around to prepare for Yab Yum position

Figure 3.9. Soft entry for Peaceful Passion: Yab Yum position

Peaceful Passion Without Intercourse

Occasionally, Richard and I connect for our ten-minute daily Peaceful Passion ceremony *without* entering into intercourse at all. (This is a good method for same-sex couples.) We begin by sitting positioned in our best directions. Then we arrange ourselves so that Richard can place one hand on my heart center and the other on my yoni, his fingers making gentle contact with both clitoris and G-spot. I place my hands on his heart and lingam. One way to accomplish this is for me to lie on my back while he kneels at my side. We don't always manage to touch each other in all the areas, but the intention is there. You might notice that this is similar to the Heart and Sex Ceremony introduced earlier in the book (see page 89). We provide enough stimulation to one another to raise the sexual energy, but mostly we simply gaze into each other's eyes, saying, "Sex," "Heart," and "Bindi." We acknowledge each location and the delicious experience evoked when we join together in this way.

Conclusion of Peaceful Passion

You might find yourself wondering…how does Peaceful Passion end? How do you know when this delightful and energizing sexual meditation is over, particularly if there's no ejaculation?

In meditation groups, the ringing of a bell can signal the end of a sitting session. But there's nobody around to ring the bell for us when we are embracing each other in a Peaceful Passion position. We're on our own.

When one of us realizes that our planned time is up, or for whatever other reason we want to end the session, we say to the other, just as in Tantra Tai Chi, "Three more." This is a reminder to focus our shared attention as fully as possible. We then take ourselves through the sex/heart/bindi pattern three more times.

We take turns saying, "Sex" and "Heart" as we squeeze and relax our sex muscles and breathe into our heart. We say, "Bindi" when we get a rush of orgasmic feeling. Obviously, this is all subjective. "Three more" might mean something completely different to Richard than it does to me. It is not an exact science! But as we reach an agreed-upon separating moment, we slowly ease apart. Sometimes, even if he entered into Peaceful Passion without an erection, Richard might be erect when he withdraws. There's an ancient Taoist saying, "In soft, out hard."

We completely disentangle and separate our bodies, actually sitting up, facing each other once again while positioned in our best directions. This is a very special moment, a moment that emphasizes sacred presence. We take time to notice how we feel as the energy of love settles into both of our bodies. We honor one another with a bow from the heart, a namasté.

RICHARD SAYS *When we first starting doing Peaceful Passion, ending the practice without ejaculating was difficult for me, although not so much from a physical perspective. There was no congestion in my groin, no blue balls, since I was moving the sexual energy up to my heart. But the* *mental habit of expecting to ejaculate during intercourse was not so easy to break. Separating and bowing to each other at the end helps reduce the desire to ejaculate. Don't forget that part!*

Even if, instead of Peaceful Passion, we had engaged in more active, rajasic sex, with climax and ejaculation, or even if our sexual time together had involved some discomfort, disappointment, or difficulty, we still sit up after it is over and share this heart salutation.

It may feel challenging for you or your partner to rouse yourself for namasté at the end of lovemaking. But you may find, as we certainly have, that it is always well worth the effort.

Yin and Yang

Mars was the Roman god of war; Venus was the goddess of love. Men and women are often seen as opposites, but I prefer to think of us as a pair. Pairs are in relationship with one another. The concept of pairs appears in almost all human stories, myths, and spiritual literature. Everyone is familiar with Adam and Eve and the later two-by-two boarding of Noah's ark. Our lives are filled with paired opposites or complementary qualities, such as giving/receiving, day/night, fire/water, inside/outside, slow/fast, wet/dry, earth/sky. All of these are embraced and explained within the classic philosophy of yin and yang.

A Story of Yin and Yang

Long ago, ancient Chinese philosophers observed and studied the ebb and flow, the increase and decline of nature in all of her magnificent manifestations. They saw that each morning the sun rose in the east, casting its brilliant light upon the landscape. They noticed, however, that only the side of a mountain facing the rising sun could receive the morning light. They called this sunny side of the mountain *yang*. The name they gave to the side of the mountain still in darkness was *yin*.

Even as the rest of earth became visible, the yin remained shrouded in darkness, its features unexposed, hidden from sight. Yang stood out bright and clear, visible to whomever wanted to see what was going on. While yang awakened to the sun's warmth, heating up from the tops of trees down to the roots in the ground, yin remained cool with nighttime dampness.

The giving and receiving of pleasure is a need and an ecstasy.
KAHLIL GIBRAN,
The Prophet

On the yang side of the mountain, leaves unfurled and turned toward the sun, drying off as they reached outward toward the light. On the yin side of the mountain, leaves and flowers remained folded in upon themselves, perhaps gathering strength or seeking an inward comfort.

There was great stirring and much movement to be seen on the yang side of the mountain, as animals awakened, stretched, and began their day. On the yin side, there was less activity, less movement, a pervasive hush across the land.

Yang continued to warm up, not just absorbing the sun's radiation, but also giving off its own heat, the heat of life, the passion of the hunt. The inhabitants, both human and animal, could be seen searching for food to bring the fire of life into their bellies and heat up their primal drives.

All the while, except perhaps for some night prowlers and night-blooming flowers, the yin side remained quiet and still, unseen.

The ancients continued to observe and saw that this great distinction between the sunny side of the mountain and the shady side of the mountain was a temporary condition. As the sun reached its zenith and began to descend toward the western horizon, that which had been in darkness now became bathed in light, and that which had been brightened was now receding into a dim obscurity. What had been yin was becoming yang, and vice versa.

What had been the sunny side of the mountain was turning into darkness. What had been hidden on the shady side was now revealed by light. The yang activity was closing down into the stillness of yin. What had been yin was expanding and awakening into the brightness of yang. The ancients looked beyond the mountain and concluded that the entire nature of the universe could be described in terms of these two ever-changing principles: yin and yang.

They began to assign characteristics to these two aspects of life, to apply the principles of yin and yang to all of the observable qualities in the universe. They described yang in terms of its brightness, its outwardly moving energy. Yang came to represent various aspects of light. That which seemed dark was called yin. Yang was warm and dry; yin was cool and moist. Yang was associated with all that was visible, the activities of daytime, the paths that could be seen to be going somewhere. Without light, the world of yin was considered secretive, less direct, more turned in upon itself.

The ancients looked at our human bodies and saw that the male sexual organs were visible and outwardly protruding. Female genitals were hidden, recessed, mysterious, and dark. Gender qualities were added to the growing catalog of what was yang and what was yin. Yang was labeled masculine and yin became the domain of the feminine.

In the cultural climate of ancient China, men were the doers, the hunters and warriors, the adventurers, the aggressors. Women stayed together, close to their shelters, were less assertive, and had children to care for and nourish. Yin came to represent that which is caring and compassionate, connected to others. Male relationships were more task-oriented, often competitive. Leadership was understood to be yang, embodied in the bodies of men. Women were described as yin, mysterious and modest. Women may have wielded power, but they had to sit behind a screen when speaking in public. They were not permitted to be seen by men, other than their husband. They were not allowed to stand in the daylight and direct the affairs of humanity.

Times have changed. Women have come out from behind the screen. Some of us women are clearly as aggressive as men. Women can wrestle and kickbox. While some women are stay-at-home moms, others are heads of states and corporations, and still others manage to do an amazing balancing act.

It is acceptable today for men to stay home to care for children, and it has become acceptable—and perhaps even expected—for them to be sensitive and affectionate. Men are not limited to playing out the yang role any more than women must remain demure and modest.

Yet the emotional yearning for deep intimate bonding with another human being can still be considered a yin attribute, whether recognized in the heart of a man or a woman. The physical desire for sexual release, the driving force of physical attraction can be considered to be yang, whether arising in the body of a man or a woman.

It is the merging of these desires, the coming together of the yin and the yang within each of us, that elevates a lovemaking experience to its highest evolution.

Deep within all of our hearts lies a profound yearning to both give love and to receive love. Jewish Kabbalah mystics describe the physical world as a vessel for receiving the light of divine love. And within this physical world, we humans have been endowed with the power to shine back that same love. We are both the givers and receivers of divine light.

Our yang ability to radiate the brightness of love is paralleled by our equally extraordinary yin ability to receive love. Sometimes it seems that we wear ourselves out trying to live up to one of these divine gifts, while ignoring the other. We sometimes give too much or too little. We are often out of balance. We may be shining our divine light into the hearts of others, but perhaps we have closed down the boundaries to our own heart, limiting access to the very treasure that we yearn to share.

In sexual love, we both extend (yang) and receive (yin). Even our anatomy blends these two principles. We each have both external and internal pleasure places. While a man appears to be primarily yang and a woman primarily yin, the fullness of lovemaking allows and creates transformation: back and forth, yang to yin and yin to yang. These dynamic forces are always interactive, always moving in relation to one another. And they are always changing. Yin and yang are linked together in a dance of balance and change.

Within our individual personalities and preferences, our unique balance of yin and yang gives us strength and authenticity. When we are too yin, we are unable stand in our own truth. When we are too yang, we are unable to make room for our partner's truth.

The Tantra Tai Chi Yin Yang Move (see next page), and the related sexual practices, help you cultivate each of these aspects by taking turns as the giver and the receiver. Although we often think of giving as a feminine trait, giving is actually a yang attribute because it has outward direction. Some of us, male or female, are natural givers; others are not. For many of us, both male and female, it is often more challenging to be the receiver, to really receive, to really let go of control by allowing our partner to be the giver, to be fully yang.

By separating into the roles of yin and yang, receiver and giver, we intensify the experience for each partner and restore ourselves to a balance of both.

The Yin Yang Move

The Yin Yang Move creates a ceremonial flow of give-and-take, based upon a grounded sense of being within one's own self. Moving in sync with your partner, you will shift toward and away from each other in an ongoing harmonious pat-

From you,
I receive,
to you, I give.
Together we share
and from this we live.
NATHAN L. SEGAL,
rabbi and songwriter

tern. The key here is to remain centered above your own feet, even as you are engaged with your partner.

When I do the Yin Yang Move with Richard, I sense-feel as if my body has a column within it, with the heart center aligned above my sex center. As I move forward and backward, as my hands flow forward and backward, the column stays upright. I am aware both of the column within me and of my connection with Richard.

When I shift my weight onto my back foot, I make space for Richard to flow his energy toward me. I am yin, receiving. As my weight shifts to my front foot, my energy flows toward him. I am yang, extending.

How to Do the Yin Yang Move

❖ Begin in Solo Stillness (see page 48), with your eyes closed. Place your awareness at the bottoms of your feet, as you sense-feel roots going down into the earth.

❖ Squeeze and release your sex muscles (see page 68).

❄ Open your eyes. When you have eye contact with your partner, step sideways together into Connected Pose (see page 55).

❄ Maintain the energy connection and keep your hands relaxed and open, palms facing toward your partner's hands.

❄ Both partners shift their weight onto the left foot and step backward with the right foot. Readjust for comfort and balance, keeping your belly buttons pointed toward each other.

❄ Sink down slightly, settling into your own hips, as if you were making yourself just a bit shorter.

❄ Partner #1: Shift more of your weight onto your front (left) foot, with your front knee slightly bent.

❄ Partner # 2: Staying upright, shift most of your weight onto your back (right) foot, with your back knee slightly bent.

❄ Each partner then shifts their body weight to their opposite foot, as each partner simultaneously moves toward or away from the other partner (see Figure 4.1).

❄ Maintain a steady rhythm, and repeat the exercise nine times.

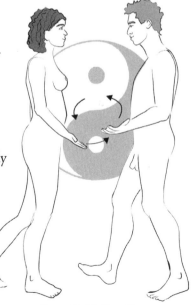

Figure 4.1. Yin Yang Move

❧ Maintain eye gaze and keep your focus on your pelvic floor.

❧ Return to Connected Pose, pausing for a moment. Then reverse feet—step back with your left foot so your right foot is forward—and repeat.

❧ After nine repetitions of the back-and-forth movements, return to Solo Stillness.

❧ When your eyes are open, return to Connected Pose and conclude with a namasté bow.

Variation with Hand Movements

As you continue the Yin Yang Move, your hands can flow toward your partner and backward to your self, making continuous circles of energy that connect your sex centers and your heart centers. When you move forward, your hands flow toward your partner; you are yang. When you shift to your back foot, your hands flow backward toward yourself; you are yin.

Partner # 1:

❧ As you shift your weight forward, let your hands flow outward from your hips, your sex center, toward your partner's sex center, and move upward to your partner's heart.

❧ As your weight shifts backward, continue the hand movement back toward your own heart center and down to your own sex center.

❧ As you shift your weight forward again, continue the hand movement back toward your partner's sex center and upward again to your partner's heart.

Partner #2:

❖ As you shift your weight backward, receive your partner's flow of energy toward your sex center. Let your hands move upward toward your heart.

❖ As your weight shifts forward, your hands move outward toward your partner's heart and downward toward their sex center.

❖ As you shift your weight backward again, continue the hand movement back toward your own sex center and upward again to your own heart.

❖ Reverse positions.

RICHARD SAYS *I enjoy visualizing moving my sexual energy flowing outward toward Diana's yoni and up to her heart. Then again, I enjoy receiving her sexual energy flowing in toward my lingam, and up to my heart. Back and forth, it is a great practice and very sensual.*

Yin and Yang in the Bedroom

Applying the principles of yin and yang in the bedroom can open new arenas for sensual pleasure. The body is the doorway to the divine, and sexuality provides a key to opening that door. Understanding—and enjoying—our individual sexual anatomy allows us to more clearly shine the light of love on the mystery of this creative force.

Sexual knowledge and wisdom attained thousands of years ago in Eastern cultures lay dormant for centuries. Many of us, fondling our beloved, have really been fumbling in the dark, often literally. Tantra invites us to make love with the lights on and to have clarity of awareness in everything, including our yin and yang genitals.

We don't have to know all the details of sexual functioning to enjoy our sexuality, any more than we need to understand the complete digestive process to enjoy a gourmet meal. But some anatomical facts are useful to increase joy and understanding of the experience. And it is fun to explore *all* the parts of our partner's body.

Our sexual features vary as much as our facial features. We are each unique. A large, small, or even crooked penis, a vulva with hidden or protruding lips, a clitoris that's close or far away from the vaginal opening—are all "normal" and worthy of our own and our beloved's appreciation and respect.

The sexual massage ceremonies presented in this section provide an opportunity for each partner to fully focus on the other, separately, for an extended period of time. These are not "quickies," so they are not meant to be undertaken as a ten-minute daily practice. Embodying the principles of Tantra Tai Chi during these longer sessions, you will help each other learn to more fully and easily activate the flow of energy between the sex and heart centers, and together share in the expanded bliss of bindi.

RICHARD SAYS *Our occasional investment of time in this manner provides a powerful foundation on which our ten-minute daily practice rests.*

The Yin Massage Ceremony

The Yin Massage Ceremony honors and celebrates the woman as yin, the receiver. The man, or giver, is yang. Yet nothing in this universe remains all yin or all yang. Even if we wanted to, we cannot choose to be 100 percent one or the other, yang or yin. At the moment of fullness, each always turns into the other. The white dot on the yin side of the symbol represents the emergence of yang energy. The dark dot on the yang side symbolizes the yin.

I am the ocean, the ocean is me. I am the goddess, I am the sea. Everything opens, as I open me. Everything opens, as I open me.
AUTHOR
UNKNOWN

Tantra, in a seeming reversal of yin-feminine-receptive and yang-masculine-active, uses the name *Shakti* to describe feminine sexual energy as a powerful, active force. The masculine is *Shiva*, the more receptive holder of spacious consciousness. It is said that the pouring forth of Shakti from a woman is necessary to ignite the male. Men really do get high seeing their partner happy, especially if it might be due to the sexual attention they have given her.

As a woman receives this hour-long massage, her continuing relaxation allows her to become more and more receptive, more and more fully yin. Eventually, her yang sexual energy, her Shakti, will burst forth.

Her partner is exhibiting the yang quality of being a focused giver. He is outward oriented. However, as his partner experiences a shift from the receptive yin to the active Shakti, he becomes a receiver of her powerful sexual force and is himself transformed. The Yin Massage can be an incredibly joyful, erotic, and fulfilling experience for both partners.

Slow Down

Women are often likened to crock pots; we heat up slowly and cook for a long time. Most men are more like microwaves, quick to heat and complete. In the beginning of a relationship, during the courting phase, the strength of your attraction for one another often overrides these differences.

RICHARD SAYS *Slowing down is so significant. If there was one thing I could recommend to men, relative to pleasing their women, it would be to slow down.*

As a couple becomes more routine in their lovemaking, timing often adjusts to the busy schedule of life and the faster pace of the male sexual pattern. Many women find themselves unable to successfully communicate their own sexual needs. They often settle for mediocre experiences or lose interest in the whole endeavor.

When a woman is given enough time and attention, she can discover deep aspects of her innate sexual experience. The Yin Massage Ceremony provides that time. In addition to the possibility of intense pleasure, the massage encourages a woman to consciously relax her pelvic floor muscles and allow the flow of sexual energy to reach her heart more readily. This also increases intimacy and trust between the partners.

Many women have had extremely negative and devastating sexual experiences such as incest, rape, or other violent assault. Even if she herself has not, the high prevalence of such experiences affects us all. And, even with a most trusted and loved partner, the odds are very high that a woman has had sexual intercourse at times when she would rather not have, and that her yoni has sometimes been entered before she was quite ready. Most common of all, she has likely had sexual intercourse *end* before she was ready for it to end.

The yoni has been both attacked and abandoned, sometimes with malice, more often out of ignorance. This loving massage can help relieve and potentially help heal the yoni of all the tension it may be carrying from a history (her-story) of such abuse or neglect.

To give the woman ample time to relax, we suggest that you allow at least an hour for the whole ceremony.

Ceremonial Attitude

It is important that no expectations are brought to this practice. This is not about "making her come" or "giving" her an orgasm. Women tend to be less goal-oriented in their sexuality than men, and they may feel pushed by their partner to emphasize orgasm. She should never be pressured, only loved. His role is to be ceremonially present and attentive, supportive of her deepening relaxation and sexual awakening.

Be sure not to schedule this time right after dinner. After a heavy dinner, especially one including alcohol consumption, it is usually more difficult to garner the conscious focus needed. Like the Tantra Tai Chi moves themselves, this is an eyes-open practice.

Also, you will want to be sure of your privacy, so that you will not be unexpectedly interrupted by children or phone calls. Turn off your phones, lock your doors. Get a babysitter. Go to a motel. Do whatever it takes to give yourselves the advantage of privacy in your sacred space.

You might like to bathe or shower together prior to this ceremony. He will want to have massage oil and personal lubricant ready, within reach. The space should be set up with enough pillows so that you will each be comfortable.

We put time into things that matter to us, things that are important. We use ceremony to honor events that matter to us, things that are sacred. Giving attention to preparing, and giving attention to the activity itself, demonstrates to one another that your time together is important, especially when you lead busy lives.

The Yin Massage draws on many of the other practices described earlier in this book. Although it is primarily about the yoni, it is not only about the yoni.

Beginning the Massage Ceremony

Giving the Yin Massage a ceremonial beginning sets the tone for a sacred sexual journey together. Sit facing one another, positioned in your best directions (see page 40). The man goes first, speaking from his heart, telling her how excited and happy he is—if that's true—about having this opportunity to pleasure and honor her. However, if he also has concerns about his skills or his ability to stay focused, he mentions these as well. He speaks his truth, simply and without excuses. She listens and does not interrupt, criticize, or correct. He can even just say, "I am here." That's what really matters, after all.

Then she replies, speaking her own truth. She may be feeling excitement, fear, curiosity, doubt, or any number or combination of emotions. At the start of a Yin Massage, I've more than once told Richard that there's a part of me that's not at all excited to be there. I could name a dozen other things I could instead be doing. But another part of me remembers how wonderful this intimate experience has been in the past, and although I'm not yet into it, I am willing to participate and see where it takes me.

Neither partner attempts to change or soothe the other person's feelings; both just listen and stay present as each states their truth. After you have both spoken, you might like to honor one another with a heart salutation. Namasté.

To start the massage, the woman lies on her back, allowing him space to sit between her legs, which extend over his. Before approaching the yoni, however, he will help her relax her whole body. Richard and I are different in how we like to be approached. He usually doesn't mind if I touch his lingam before touching any other body part. Most of the men in our workshops agree. Like me, most of the women would recoil from such a direct charge on the yoni. An abrupt touch on the clitoris can be uncomfortable and even feel like an attack.

So the massage proceeds slowly, and although this practice is often called a "yoni massage," it doesn't start right between her legs. He rests his hands gently on her torso, her heart center, belly, thighs. Looking into each other's eyes, the couple breathes together, connecting the sex and heart centers. Remember the Heart and Sex Ceremony (see page 89).

He then begins to softly stroke her entire body, including the yoni but not focusing on it yet. Long gentle strokes from the knees, up to the chest area. If she likes, he can use oil or lotion on her skin. For the inner tissues of the yoni itself, it is safer to use a water-based personal lubricant or natural substance that she is already comfortable with.

I love when Richard's fingers graze across my yoni as he caresses my body. I feel the stirring of erotic feelings in my whole body.

With his palms or fingertips, the man caresses his partner's inner and outer thighs and her belly. He lets his fingertips graze her yoni as his hands slowly slide and glide up and down her body (see Figure 4.2 on the next page). She is his guide, letting him know what feels good, how she would like him to touch her,

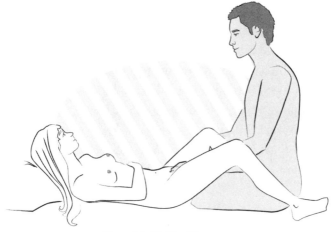

Figure 4.2. Yin/Yoni Massage

how much pressure and where. She might like him to massage or make circles around her breasts or nipples.

Sometimes I ask Richard to reach all the way down to my ankles.

Giving Guidance—Men DO Like Directions

Most couples need more practice in giving each other directions regarding touch. Maybe we're afraid to hurt our partner's feelings, or we feel it is inappropriate. And there's that genetic thing about men not asking for directions. They actually do like having directions. They just don't like to ask for them.

Communicating desires is a skill that you and your partner can practice together. Communication can certainly be challenging. During lovemaking with Richard, when he was delightfully pleasuring me orally, I would say to him, "Oh, that's so great!"

Moments later, I noticed that it didn't feel as fabulous and I'd find myself squirming about for better placement. When we finally talked about it, we learned that when I said, "That's great!" to Richard, his male brain translated it to mean, "Good job, well done, on to something else." He figured he was done with that and would move on to another spot or change the rhythm or tempo. What I really meant—and now know to say directly—was, "Oh, that's so great, keep doing it, don't change a thing, stay right where you are, and continue doing exactly what you're doing!"

As you enjoy this Yin Massage Ceremony, be as specific as you possibly can with the directions and guidance you give to your partner.

Speaking Tantra Tai Chi

Using the language of Tantra Tai Chi during the massage, occasionally saying, "Sex," "Heart," or "Bindi" to each other, heightens the tantric experience. Eye contact is maintained throughout, even though it is often easier to focus on sensations when the eyes are closed. Sometimes I tell Richard that I'm going to close my eyes now for a bit. But this is a ceremony of intimacy, and after a while, I will open them again, or Richard will gently say, "Eyes," to me, to bring me back to the shared experience.

Sometimes I ask for a pause or for Solo Stillness. Of course, we don't stand up in the Tantra Tai Chi position. Richard's hands continue to rest on me, as we each settle into our own selves, knowing that we are not distancing from one another by doing so. Hands are still, eyes are closed. Eventually we open our eyes and say, "Eyes" to invite the other back into the visual connection.

After a comfortable amount of time caressing the legs, torso, and breasts, it will be time for him to focus more specifically on the yoni. He will check with her, because all timing is up to her during this practice. This first part of the massage can last as little as five minutes or even as long as fifteen minutes.

When she's ready, with her permission, he now begins to focus more specifically on the yoni, stroking the outer and inner lips/labia (see Figure 4.3 on the next page). Even if she is moist, it is a good idea to use personal lubricant. He might try long, slow strokes, from the bottom of the yoni opening up toward the clitoris, ending with circles around the clitoris, without actually touching it at first. He might roll or caress one side of the yoni in his fingers and then the other. She is his guide, letting him know what feels good, where to stay, and how fast or slow to go. Guiding a lover is a new experience for most women, and it can take some time to get over any embarrassment. There's no rush, no hurry.

The Clitoris

The clitoris (see Figure 4.3 on the next page) is a sensitive organ that packs a big punch when it comes to erotic arousal. Thanks to research and reports beginning in the mid-1960s, the world awoke to a recognition of the clitoris as a woman's most exciting sexual organ. There had been, and often still is, an expectation that the in-and-out thrusting of penis-in-vagina is the only way, or the best way, for a woman to experience orgasm. The role of the clitoris had been, and often still is, overlooked.

Did you know that the clitoris isn't *just* that small bud (or not so small), resting under the hood formed by the inner labia? It is shaped more like a wishbone, with hidden legs that extend several inches back into the yoni area.

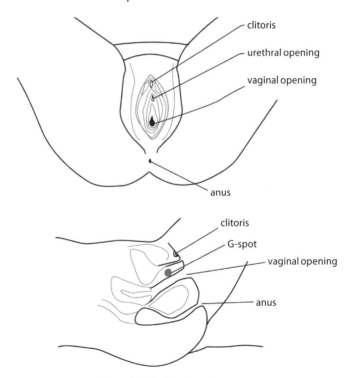

Figure 4.3. The female anatomy

Did you know that the clitoris develops prior to any masculinization of the human fetus? Under the influence of the male chromosome, the clitoris legs join together to form the cavities of a penis. In a woman, these legs, still separated, are made of erectile tissue that can become aroused when caressed. The clitoris stands alone as a body part that has no function other than pleasure!

Did you know that after a climax, the clitoris may awaken sexual response again, and again, but it also may withdraw from direct touch or be too sensitive for the same intensity of stimulation?

The Yin Massage Ceremony provides time for you and your partner to explore all facets of the clitoral area. Experiencing climax is not the goal of the massage, although one—or more— may certainly occur. There are no rules; you can enjoy yourself as much as you like. You are not required to have a climax, nor are you required to forego having one or more of them.

Breathe!

As arousal builds, we women tend to hold our breath and use fantasy or other mental intention to focus directly on the sexual stimulation in order for us to "reach" climax. In this massage, it is best to just relax and breathe out, using the Tantra Tai Chi pattern of moving energy between the sex and heart centers and keeping eye contact with your partner. The relaxation of the pelvic muscles may actually result in even greater orgasms with less effort.

At first, the breathing and relaxing may seem to take focus away from the erotic genital sensations, but eventually your attention is recaptured at a deeper level. While Richard massages me, I often create a continuous rhythm of tightening and releasing my sex muscles, along with my breath. I use my hands to sweep the energy upward, to bring attention to my heart, as in the Tantra Tai Chi Heart Move (see page 86). I treasure the shift to bindi when it occurs.

One of my favorite things to do during the Yin Massage, while I am tightening and releasing those sex muscles, is to say, "Oooh" and "Aaah," just as I suggested to you in the Tantra Tai Chi Sex Move (see page 74). I say, "Oooh," when I squeeze the sex muscles, and I say, "Aaah," when I relax. "Oooh." "Aaah." Over and over again.

Experiment with breathing out with the "aaah" sound as you consciously relax the yoni area. If your yoni muscles are a little too tight, you can even relax without squeezing, as if simply letting go, with a little downward or outward push, like starting on the first floor of an elevator, and moving downward.

As your partner massages and pleasures the outer and inner areas of the yoni, communicate what feels good and could feel even better, now, in this moment. "Oooh." "Aaah."

Inside the Yoni

After five to fifteen minutes of caressing and stimulating the clitoris and outer yoni area, if she has not already invited him to do so, the man can ask if it would be a good time for him to enter her yoni with his finger. It is always good to *verbally* request permission before entry. Or she can invite him in whenever she wants.

Using additional lubrication, he slowly and gradually enters her yoni with his middle finger while still caressing the outer area with his other hand. Or she might prefer a thumb or two or three fingers. (Make sure his nails are trimmed and he has no hangnails!)

She continues to squeeze and relax her sex muscles even as he moves into this phase of the massage. She breathes and says, "Oooh" and "Aaah," as if doing the Tantra Tai Chi Sex and Heart Moves.

The inner area of the yoni is then fully massaged, all 360 degrees, back and front, with a firm circular stroke all around. He can use his right hand to massage the right side of the yoni and his left hand for the left side. He can vary the pressure and the pattern of the stroke. Be sure to add or request enough personal lubricant.

This massage is both healing and erotic. Like any other part of the body, some areas within the yoni may feel tight when massaged. If she notices discomfort or pain at anytime, she asks him to pause, to lighten his pressure. Sometimes just keeping a finger on the area and looking into one another's eyes can bring enormous relief.

Relief sometimes expresses itself as emotional release, and she may cry, scream, or perhaps laugh delightedly. He allows her to express herself without trying to fix or change her reaction, which is part of the healing process. Both partners continue to maintain eye contact, squeeze and relax the sex muscles, and breathe into the heart.

During this somewhat "clinical" massage of the inner yoni, his other hand can continue to simulate the clitoris and outer area—which makes it quite pleasurable and not so "clinical" at all. Always maintain a sense of honoring one another.

Sacred Spot

After massaging the whole yoni area, the man begins to feel along the front wall of his partner's yoni for her G-spot (see Figure 4.3 on page 154). In Tantra this spot is often called her sacred spot or sacred gate.

I call my clitoris my "outer goddess" and my G-spot my "inner goddess." The G-spot is an area within the front vaginal wall, behind the clitoris and pubic bone, that responds erotically to deep pressure. It was named after a pioneering gynecologist, Dr. Gräfenberg, who described it to unbelieving medical colleagues in 1950. Although found in ancient Eastern teachings, it wasn't until the 1980s that Western literature became available concerning this anatomical feature of women.

Did you know that the G-spot is not really a spot but an area filled with glandular tissue? Previously called paraurethral glands or Skene's glands, the G-spot is now thought of as the "female prostate." If the male Y chromosome had been present in the development of life, this tissue would have become a prostate gland. It is possible that the amount of testosterone in a developing female baby determines how large or small this area becomes.

Did you know that when this area is deeply massaged, it becomes engorged and can release a fluid similar to the pre-ejaculate fluid of men? Different from vaginal moisture in taste and consistency, ancient Tantra texts call this sweet fluid *amrita*, or "nectar of the goddess." It is excreted directly into the urethra, and it may even exit the body as an ejaculation.

Without up-to-date sexual knowledge, many women have thought they were accidentally urinating instead of recognizing and enjoying the fluid as a sign of sexual release and spiritual opening. For a comprehensive explanation of female ejaculation, see *Female Ejaculation & the G-Spot* by Deborah Sundahl.

Locating and Pleasuring the G-Spot

The tissue along the walls of the yoni is usually smooth. The area indicating the G-spot has a rougher texture. It is located on the front wall of the vagina, from a half-inch to two inches up toward the stomach. It may be as small as the pad of a pinky, or much larger, especially if she has already had stimulation and climax. Just touching or lightly stroking this area may not feel particularly erotic or pleasurable.

Substantial pressure is required to create any sensations. It is not the rough area itself that is the G-spot, but the firmer tissue behind it. To deeply massage the G-spot, he hooks either one or two fingers, using a "come here" stroke with firm pressure, up into the spongy tissue, and then toward the front, and side to side.

RICHARD SAYS *Stimulating the G-spot takes a lot more pressure than I would have thought. You have to really press up into the area—often more than an inch. If you just touch it lightly, she won't feel a thing.*

Because the urethra runs through this area, women often feel the urge to urinate when the G-spot is massaged. This can be a very uncomfortable feeling at first, but, if she continues to squeeze and relax her sex muscles, "Ooohing" and "Aaahing" and breathing into the heart, the discomfort or urge to urinate can transform into a very heightened experience of sexual release.

When the G-spot is massaged deeply, the resulting orgasmic experience can be quite different from that which comes from clitoral stimulation alone. Dr. Beverly Whipple, one of the original authors of the first book about the G-spot, has since published *The Science of Orgasm*, explaining in detail how the brain is involved in women's sexual response. The nerve structure that connects the G-spot to the brain takes an entirely different pathway than from the clitoris. This means that the experience of orgasm may also be noticeably different, depending on where stimulation is received. Many women enjoy orgasm that arises from simultaneous stimulation.

During this extended massage, as the woman continues to relax, she can guide her partner to provide more stimulation of her "outer goddess" or more pressure on her "inner goddess" or both at the same time. She can request that he just be still, maintaining eye contact, as they share the moment. Each woman can use this time to experiment and discover her own body's wisdom.

Moving to Her Side

For the final portion of the Yin Massage, Richard likes to move to my side (See Figure 4.4). In this position he has closer eye contact with me, and also finds it a comfortable way to access both my inner and outer goddesses.

In addition, he enjoys resting into hand positions that allow both of us to more fully integrate the high energy of this ceremonial massage. He likes to think of these hand positions as

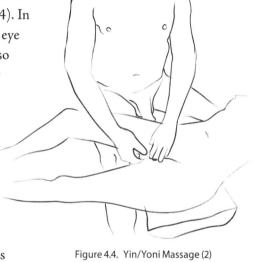

Figure 4.4. Yin/Yoni Massage (2)

mudras, bringing in a sense of the spiritual. Sometimes he keeps pressure on my G-spot while his other hand rests on my pubic Mound of Venus or on or near my clitoris. He senses energy from the G-spot flowing up his arm, through his heart, and back down his other arm to my body.

It gives me the opportunity to focus on the connection between my outer and inner sources of vibrational charge.

Sometimes he settles into holding my heart and sex, as in the Heart and Sex Ceremony (see page 89), while we gaze at each other, once again saying, "Heart," "Sex," and "Bindi," to each other.

Of course, when a man sits at the side of his beloved, naked, there is a strong temptation for her to begin reciprocal pleasuring. However, to continue this experience as a Yin Massage Ceremony, it is best to refrain and to keep the focus fully on her as receiver, him as giver.

Concluding the Yin Massage Ceremony

The Yin Massage Ceremony continues for about an hour, until she feels it is over. It doesn't end because she has an orgasm, and it doesn't need to continue until she has an orgasm. There are no rules other than being loving with one another, staying focused in both the sex and heart centers, and celebrating bindi.

The Yin Massage is not foreplay, nor is it sexual activity intended to lead to intercourse. Actually, I don't know why a woman's pleasuring time is so often called foreplay, when for many women, it is the most completely satisfying aspect of the sexual encounter. Be sure to treat the Yin Massage as a rewarding sexual ceremony in and of itself. When it is over, sit up, face one another, and honor each another with a heart salutation. Namasté.

RICHARD SAYS *Pleasuring Diana as she enjoys climaxes and orgasms is pleasure for me. Spending a whole hour "serving" her in this way is awesome. I can't begin to describe how* *much I enjoy it. Seeing my wife naked and happy, responding to my touch, is about as good as it gets.*

Yin/Yoni Massage Reminders

The following lists will help you and your partner each remember what to focus on during the Yin/Yoni Massage Ceremony. These suggestions are intended to enhance the experience for both of you. Ignore whatever does not do that. Each time you engage in this sexual ceremony, you will discover and create your own favorite ways of enjoying it.

For Her: Yin Massage Reminders

- ❊ Establish an "I am here" heart-space with your lover.
- ❊ Briefly tell him how you are feeling in this moment.
- ❊ Keep eye contact throughout.
- ❊ Give appropriate feedback and guidance—direct his hands, ask for more lubrication, and so forth.
- ❊ Remind yourself to relax and breathe.
- ❊ Vocalize, "Oooh" (like the *ou* in "you") as you squeeze your yoni muscles and "Aaah" as you relax or push out.
- ❊ Take time to sense-feel, doing the Sex, Heart, and Bindi Moves; say the words aloud.
- ❊ Ask for Solo Stillness if desired. Say, "Eyes" to reconnect.
- ❊ Allow yourself to feel adored and worshipped by your lover.
- ❊ At conclusion, sit facing each other for namasté.

For Him: Yin Massage Reminders

❖ Establish an "I am here" heart-space with your lover.

❖ Briefly tell her how you are feeling in this moment.

❖ Sit between her legs, and begin the massage by holding both her heart and sex centers.

❖ Massage and relax her body for five to fifteen minutes, *including*—but not focusing on—the yoni itself. Invite her to make requests and give you guidance. Massage oil may be used.

❖ After the body massage, or at her request, focus on slowly pleasuring the yoni, clitoris, vaginal lips, and so forth for at least five to fifteen minutes. Use personal lubricant.

❖ Ask permission to enter her yoni with your finger(s), or do so at her request. Enter slowly.

❖ Slowly massage the internal area of the yoni, using small circular movements, 360 degrees around. Use lubrication.

❖ Next, focus specifically on the G-spot (feel for a rough area). Apply significant pressure with a "come-here" finger movement, and also use your finger to move from side to side on her G-spot.

❖ Continue, with her guidance, pleasuring her clitoris ("outer goddess") along with her G-spot ("inner goddess").

❖ Keep eye contact throughout. Say, "Eyes!" as appropriate.

❖ Let her know if you start feeling uncomfortable physically; ask if it is okay to readjust your sitting position.

❧ Move to her side, continuing to honor her inner and outer goddesses. Hold your hands still at times, one hand on each. Feel the *Shakti* energy flow through you.

❧ Hold her heart with one hand while the other holds both G-spot and clitoris.

❧ At conclusion, sit facing each other for namasté.

The Yang Massage Ceremony

In the Yang Massage, the man is the receiver. It is approached in the same slow, ceremonial, sacred manner as the Yin Massage. It is similar in many other ways as well. It is an opportunity for the man to relax into his yin nature, to totally relax and receive. When I first tried this with Richard, he had a hard time not taking back the giver role—he kept wanting to touch and pleasure me. Although mutual stimulation during lovemaking is delightful, the sexual massage ceremonies are most effective when the yin/yang roles are clearly defined and adhered to.

RICHARD SAYS *I didn't know how to relax into a high state of sexual arousal. Reaching out to grab Diana was my way of diffusing the energy without ejaculating. With the Tantra Tai Chi training, I have learned to breathe that energy to my heart, which has the effect of maintaining the arousal but relieving the pressure to release it just yet.*

The Yang Massage proceeds slowly, giving him lots of time to surrender into his inner self. This is not your basic "hand-job."

I recommend at least thirty to forty-five minutes for the whole experience, which, although shorter than the Yin Massage, is a long time for most men to be stimulated prior to ejaculation. It is best if couples have already experienced the Yin Massage Ceremony before doing a Yang Massage. The Yin Massage provides a framework for knowing how to proceed in this reversed situation. Although the anatomy is different, the intention and process is pretty much the same. To begin, in both massage ceremonies, sit facing each other and tell one another how you are feeling in this moment, as you are embarking on this ceremonial journey of love. Either or both of you might be excited, nervous, bored, or whatever. Yet you have both shown up and are intending to be present for the experience. Establish a sense of "I am here" by saying the words aloud to each other.

He then lays back and she sits between his legs, in the same way that he sits when giving her the Yin Massage (see Figure 4.5 on the next page). She begins with a massage of his whole body. He will appreciate her touching and stroking his lingam as she helps him to relax and to spread his sexual energy up his chest and down his legs. Remember, in the Yin Massage, women prefer long strokes on the body, before the yoni is even touched. Here, though, it is perfectly okay to start at the lingam and let the long strokes flow from there.

Keep your eyes open, and keep your hearts connected during the massage. If he becomes extremely aroused, she pauses and places a hand on his chest, reminding him to squeeze his sex

Figure 4.5. Yang/Lingam Massage

muscles and breathe the squeeze upward, as in the Tantra Tai Chi Heart and Bindi Moves. He can vocalize the "Oooh-Aaah" sounds if he likes.

RICHARD SAYS   *While receiving this massage, I particularly like doing the Tantra Tai Chi Heart Move, squeezing my sex and breathing the sexual energy into my heart and chest area.*

After five or ten minutes of full body massaging, she begins to focus even more specifically on his lingam and testicles. He may or may not have an erection during different phases of this massage. It makes no difference. The lingam can be lovingly caressed whether it is hard or flaccid.

The power of this massage is his learning to relax even while in high states of sexual arousal. It is important that he communicates to her when she must slow down or stop stimulating him so that he can delay ejaculation. This is a great exercise for him to practice becoming more conscious of his ejaculatory edge. However, if an ejaculation occurs and he prefers that the massage ends at this time, that's fine too.

RICHARD SAYS *Although ejaculation is likely and thoroughly enjoyable during or at the end of this massage, the goal is to experience the journey along the way. I had to become sensitive to my arousal levels in order to let Diana know when I was getting close to that place of "no return." Now I can more easily instruct her to stop or just hold me while I deepen my breathing from sex to heart.*

As she begins to focus more on the lingam, he can give her guidance as to what type of strokes he likes. Although the golden rule says, "Do unto others as you would have them to do unto you," it is even better to "Do unto others as they would like you to do unto them"! This is known as "the platinum rule." Women often use a softer touch than a man enjoys, while men often use too firm a touch with their partner because it might be what they themselves would generally like. A soft touch, however, might be just perfect for his testicles, which generally enjoy being gently tugged and fondled.

Hello, Prostate!

After pleasuring his lingam directly for about ten minutes, or as long as he would like—or can stand—it will be time to explore the prostate. The prostate is the organ that produces seminal fluid (see Figure 4.6 below). Like the female prostate or G-spot, it can be the source of extremely erotic experiences. Just as a woman's brain receives and responds to clitoral and G-spot stimulation differently, so does the male brain receive and respond to stimulation from the prostate in a different manner than from the penis. In addition, massage is considered particularly healthy for the male prostate.

One way to stimulate this gland is through the perineum, the soft place between his testicles and anus (see Figure 4.6 below). Some men call this "the million dollar point" and enjoy it being pressed deeply. Another approach to the prostate, generally more effective, is by direct contact through the anus.

Men who have received prostate exams from their doctor may wonder how this differs. Trust me, it does.

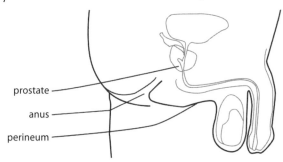

Figure 4.6. The male anatomy

A ceremonial prostate massage from his beloved partner can be an incredible experience for a man. However, if you've never given or received one, just hearing about it may bring up some concerns. If he likes it, does that mean he's gay? No! Many men and women enjoy anal touching, even anal sex, with their opposite sex partner.

Another concern might be about hygiene and the "ick factor." You can use a latex glove or finger cot, and some women even ask their partners to take a warm-water enema prior to a prostate massage. Afterward, be sure to either wash your hand or throw away your glove before touching yourself with the finger that was inside the anus.

RICHARD SAYS *Until I received this prostate massage, I only had a philosophical understanding of the principles of yin and yang. The experience of being entered in this way allowed me to empathize with my feminine aspect and brought a whole new balance to my masculinity. Also, the way I experience orgasm through prostate massage is less direct than from penile stimulation. It is even sometimes elusive, in the same way women describe their orgasms.*

Locating and Pleasuring the Prostate
Begin slowly, using lots of lubrication. Entry into the anal opening needs to be very gentle and sensually sensitive. Women must certainly take care if they have long fingernails. Once inside,

take a left & second light

there really isn't anything in the canal except his prostate. It is usually possible to reach it with a finger, although this might not be so in all cases. She may only be able to touch the bottom side of his prostate.

Once he becomes aware of her finger, the man can guide his beloved as to how much pressure to apply. Use a "come-here" motion and also massage the prostate with a side-to-side movement. He can also let her know whether to continue stimulating his lingam at the same time, or in an alternating manner.

It is especially powerful for him to tighten his pelvic floor muscles and breathe the sexual energy up to his heart or bindi, where he then breathes out and releases it. Remembering the Tantra Tai Chi moves is very helpful in slowing down and allowing him to access his deeper sexual being.

Maintain eye contact throughout the massage. He can also ask for Solo Stillness. She can hold his sex and heart and feel the energy running between them.

Continue for the allotted time or until he is ready to stop. At the end, sit up and honor one another with a namasté bow.

Yang/Lingam Massage Reminders

The following lists will help you and your partner each remember what to focus on during the Yang/Lingam Massage Ceremony. These are only suggestions, of course, and you should let yourself be guided by the merging of sex, heart, and bindi, and the powerful energy of your love.

For Her: Yang Massage Reminders

❈ Establish an "I am here" heart-space with your lover.

❈ Briefly tell him how you are feeling in this moment.

❈ Keep eye contact throughout. Say, "Eyes," as appropriate.

❈ Sit between his legs. Massage and relax his body for five to fifteen minutes, including—but not focusing on—the lingam. He can make requests and give guidance. Massage oil can be used.

❈ Use your hands to help him connect his sex and heart centers.

❈ After the body massage, or at his request, focus on the lingam, testicles, perineum, and so forth for another five to fifteen minutes.

❈ Ask permission to massage his prostate, or do so at his request. Enter slowly, using lots of lubrication.

❈ Massage the prostate, using a "come-here" finger movement and also applying pressure from side to side.

❈ Continue, with his guidance, pleasuring both his prostate and lingam.

❈ At the conclusion, sit facing each other for namasté.

For Him: Yang Massage Reminders

❈ Establish an "I am here" heart-space with your lover.

❈ Briefly tell her how you are feeling in this moment.

❈ Keep eye contact throughout.

❄ Give appropriate feedback, guidance, ask for more lubrication, and so forth.

❄ Remind yourself to relax and breathe.

❄ Squeeze your sex and breathe the energy up into your heart.

❄ Say, "Oooh" as you squeeze and, "Aaah" as you relax and open your heart. You can do this throughout the session.

❄ Sense-feel doing the Sex, Heart, and Bindi Moves; say the words aloud.

❄ Ask for Solo Stillness if desired. Say, "Eyes" to reconnect.

❄ Allow yourself to feel adored and worshipped by your lover.

❄ At conclusion, sit facing each other for namasté.

The Yin/Yang Exchange

As wonderful as the Yin and Yang Massages are, you won't always have enough time for such luxurious lovemaking. The following Yin/Yang Exchange can be enjoyed even when you have only ten minutes. In this ceremony, each of you gets to ask the other to touch or massage or pleasure you exactly how and where you would like to be touched, massaged, or pleasured. You also get to touch, massage, and pleasure your partner. You take turns being the receiver and the giver by asking each other questions, starting with either with "May I?" or "Will you?" Mixing up the giving and receiving, the yin and yang, can make a lovemaking session exciting and bring newness to each experience.

For example, your partner might say, "May I kiss your left nipple?" You would answer, "Yes!" (if you are willing to receive this), and your partner then carries out the action. After some moments, you, the receiver of the action, responds, "Thank you."

Then it is your turn to ask. You will be giving or receiving, depending on whether you begin your question with "May I" or "Will you." "Will you...kiss my other nipple?" If your partner says yes, then it is your partner who carries out the action again, and you receive. Then say, "Thank you."

"May I...caress the tip of your lingam with my tongue?" "Yes." Actions are carried out, and the receiver says, "Thank you." Back and forth you go, asking, accepting, performing the action, and thanking your partner. Always starting with "May I" or "Will you." Be sure to use both phrases during this ceremony.

RICHARD SAYS *Sometimes initiating sex play can be awkward. Starting with the Yin/Yang Exchange, giving and receiving in response to each other's requests, makes it fun and nonthreatening.*

Sometimes the Answer Is "No"

Sometimes, you or your partner may choose to answer, "No" instead of "Yes." Say, "No" when you prefer not to engage in the action or maybe you just don't want to do it at that moment. If the answer is, "No," the asking partner gets to ask again. The asker can ask for something entirely different, or simply fine-tune the original question. The new question can begin with either "May I?" or "Will you?" The same partner continues to ask until getting a "Yes" response.

Staying present and making a different request, after being told, "No," is a powerful practice. Too often in relationships, receiving a negative response can lead to an overall feeling of rejection. Sometimes you may not even realize it until later.

I remember times when Richard invited me to join him in the bedroom or physically touched me in a sex-initiating way while I was sitting at my computer or otherwise involved in a project. If I said, "No" or pushed him away because I didn't want to be disturbed at that moment, he would sometimes withdraw, maybe not even realizing that he felt rejected. Later, if I reached out to engage him in love, he might have pretended to be asleep, silently communicating in retaliation to my earlier refusal. And so cycles of pursuit and rejection can begin and continue.

Now, when we say, "No" to one another's advances, we realize it is not a total rejection, it is just a response to the request being made at the present moment. If I say, "No" or push him away, Richard now might ask if I will be available for love in half an hour, or he might ask if he can kiss the back of my neck. "Yes," I might say, and our connection remains strong—without interrupting the task that I am involved in. In the Yin/Yang Exchange, a "no" means no to that specific request at this moment, and it includes an invitation to ask again.

How Long to Play?

You can play back and forth for five or ten minutes, for half an hour, or for half a day. It is up to you and your partner.

Outside the Bedroom

This ceremonial game is great played naked in bed, with requests including specific body parts such as tongues, nipples, clitoris, yoni, testicles, lingam, anus—you name it. But it can also be played clothed, in public, even on a beach or park blanket while children are playing nearby. Hugging, touching, massaging, kissing a forehead, many loving actions can comfortably be done in public. "May I massage your left foot?" "Yes!" "Thank you."

Yin/Yang Energy Variation

This is particularly fun when you're sitting at a restaurant. Ask for something erotic that wouldn't be appropriate to do right there. For example, "Will you make three circles around my clitoris with your tongue?" But instead of actually carrying out the action, you both stay still, looking into each other's eyes as you each sense-feel, *imagine* the doing or receiving of that particular action. This neither involves nor requires actual touching, kissing, or rubbing.

Using your inner sensing to imagine experiencing one another's touch and presence is a major key to developing intimacy at a deep level. Be as detailed and sexually specific as you can. Agree that a "Yes!" in this energy game means simply that you agree to do it right now *in energy only*. It is not a promise for that specific activity at any later time.

Or while you are in sexual union, be still and invite your partner to imagine experiencing specific sensations of energy such as, "Will you send love from the tip of your lingam all the way up to my heart?" "Yes!" Then each of you senses what that flow of energy might feel like. "Thank you! May I look through your eyes into your heart?" "Yes!"

When sex is enjoyed as a **S**ynchronized **E**nergy e**X**change, you can send and receive energy back and forth and actually feel it as a vibrational reality. Exchanging the roles of yin and yang, you can guide and shape your lovemaking so it becomes an expanded experience of blended bliss.

Other Variations

- One person makes all of the requests, using both "May I?" and "Will you?" for a set period of time. The other partner's turn can follow immediately or take place on another day.

- Partners take turns, but using only "May I?" for a period of time. During a separate period of time, all the requests begin with "Will you?"

- Take turns sensually awakening and delighting one another's senses with feathers and other items of touch, various scents to smell, pieces of fruit to eat, and bells or other sounds to hear. The receiving partner might like to be blindfolded or might prefer to make specific requests. Let the Yin/Yang Exchange become a treasured and fun part of your life together.

5

A Commitment to Intimacy

A Sanskrit word for "vow" or "sacred bond," is *samaya*, used originally to refer to the relationship between guru and disciple. Conscious lovers can honor one another with the same purity of intentional commitment.

I don't commit easily, but when I do, I do. My astrological sign is Taurus, the bull, and I can be bullish in my commitments.

Richard is very different. He says, "Yes" easily but doesn't always feel it is essential to follow through on everything he says he's going to do. That's not to say that the important things don't get done. I'm talking more about announcements such as, "I'm going to the gym." An hour and a half later, I may notice he's watering the yard or answering an e-mail!

Even so, Richard has been able to commit to, and show up for, our daily practice of tantric sex, our daily ten minutes of intimate and peaceful passion. He is committed to walking the path of intimacy with me. He is unwaveringly committed to being alive in each moment. *Yes!*

RICHARD SAYS *I get so much energy and joy from our daily ten minutes of "peaceful passion" that I have no problem honoring that particular commitment!*

But all vows, all commitments, however intentional, have a way of falling by the wayside without occasional renewal. The Tantra Tai Chi Commitment Move is a fun way to renew our ongoing vow, our commitment to one another.

Not only does life often intervene and pull us away from our intentions, but sometimes we can show up and still not be 100 percent present. A verbal, ceremonial exercise called *All of Me* helps me align with my commitment, my samaya, even when something in me seems to be pulling away. I hope it will be useful for you as well.

The Commitment Move: YES!

Commitment can be a scary word. But what does it really mean? Being in a relationship implies that at some level you have both agreed to spend time together in a way that is meaningful to each of you. Successful couples meet the promise of commitment by putting their relationship on the agenda, scheduling appointments for love, and showing up.

Commitment is so important that we designed a fun, energizing Tantra Tai Chi move called—you guessed it—Commitment. In other moves, you use your voice to name a particular area of the body. In the Commitment Move, you say one word over and over. The word is "*yes*"!

Saying, "I do" in the first place may have been a big step, or may even be a step you haven't yet taken. My own response to Richard's marriage proposal was beyond hesitant—I was totally speechless. I kept opening my mouth but no words came forth. Did I really want to make this major commitment, to promise myself in body, heart, and soul to this one man? I did.

Yet even more important than that "big one" is the frequent and intentional commitment that we continue to make every day. We agree to be on this journey together, to laugh, play, cry, love, and learn together, to climb the sacred mountain, hand in hand. This intention gets expressed over and over again, in the same or different ways.

Like many women, at least those who value connection and love above all other attributes, the expression of our commitment matters to me. You've probably heard of the husband who, in response to his wife's attempt at getting a verbalization of love from him, replies, "I married you, didn't I?" For him, perhaps, the restating of love and commitment is unnecessary. For her, however, it is essential.

The Tantra Tai Chi Commitment Move gives us both a chance to say, "Yes!" without having to specify exactly what it is we're saying yes to. We can be saying yes to sex, yes to heart, yes to bindi, to our spiritual nature, yes to love. Most importantly, we are saying yes to each other, yes to our relationship, and, even more importantly, we are saying yes together.

Although you might prefer to enjoy the Commitment Move *before* the Sex, Heart, and Bindi Moves, I like it at the end for its invigorating qualities. Sometimes I even do it alone to enliven myself.

RICHARD SAYS *When I return to Solo Stillness after the exuberance of the Commitment Move, I feel a heightened sense of peace.*

How to Do the Commitment Move

As in the other Tantra Tai Chi movements, this one incorporates squeezing and releasing the sex muscles. However, unlike the others, this movement is not intended to stay slow and meditative. Allow it to speed up energetically, with robust shouts of "Yes!" with each swing of the arms.

- ❋ Begin in Solo Stillness (see page 48), with your eyes closed. Place your awareness at the bottoms of your feet as you sense-feel roots going down into the earth.

- ❋ Squeeze and release your sex muscles (see page 68).

- ❋ Open your eyes. When you have eye contact with your partner, step sideways together into Connected Pose (see page 55).

- ❋ Step back from each other to create additional space.

- ❋ Sink down slightly and remain with your height lowered.

- ❋ Swing your left hand forward, fingertips toward your lover, and swing your right hand behind you.

- ❋ Your left palm is facing your lover's left palm.

❖ Then swing your left hand behind you and swing the right hand forward, fingertips toward your lover, right palms facing each other.

❖ Arms are relaxed and remain close to body as the hands swing to the front and back.

❖ Each time your palms meet at the end of each swing (see Figure 5.1 below), say, "Yes!" and squeeze your sex muscles.

Figure 5.1. The Commitment Move

❁ Relax the sex muscles while your hands are swinging to the reverse position.

❁ Maintain eye contact throughout.

❁ After one of you says to the other, "Three more," do the final swings in slow motion, holding the palms facing each other for an extra moment or two each time.

❁ Return to Solo Stillness, bring your feet together, and close your eyes. Sense-feel your roots reaching into the ground.

❁ Notice how energized you feel.

❁ When you feel fully connected with yourself, allow your eyes to open.

❁ When your partner's eyes are open, step sideways together into Connected Pose.

❁ Complete the practice with a namasté heart salutation.

All of Me

Making a commitment to practice tantric sex might mean that you and your partner expect each other to show up at specific, mutually agreed-upon times. As you have read throughout this book, Richard and I have a commitment for at least ten minutes every day.

Sometimes, however, even though I show up at our agreed-upon time, or perhaps even in the middle of making love, I may notice that there is something in me that doesn't really want to participate. I become aware that something in me, some part of me, is reluctant, holding back. I do not feel 100 percent fully present with Richard.

Being present in the moment, the here and now, with what is, is a cornerstone of intimate, tantric loving. Not only does intimacy invite you to reveal your love, your delight in the relationship, but intimacy also invites you to reveal any part of yourself that—in this moment—may feel unloved or unloving, or just not wanting to be there. Being pulled in different directions is a common experience. Within each of us lives a multitude of parts, various fragmented aspects of ourselves. Some of these parts are familiar; others show up as a surprise. Each part seems to have its own belief system, its own way of reacting to life. Sometimes we are embarrassed by, or even ashamed of, a part of ourselves, of how that part thinks and might act. Sometimes we are aware of one part of ourselves arguing with another part, one part trying to reason with another part or trying to make it go away or become invisible.

It is so, right now.
ANN WEISER CORNELL, author of *The Radical Acceptance of Everything*

When parts of ourselves are ignored or kept hidden, a barrier can develop, preventing deeper intimacy with our partner. Yet every part of us is alive, each is part of our whole aliveness. It may not seem so, but all the parts are wanting something for us, trying to protect us or benefit us in some way. Unfortunately, their strategy for doing so may create the opposite effect, seemingly sabotaging our higher intentions for ourselves and our relationship. What if we allowed ourselves to acknowledge whatever part of us shows up, here and now, in the presence of our beloved? Acknowledging a part of ourselves does not mean agreeing with that part's point of view. Ann Weiser Cornell, who teaches the skills of Inner Relationship Focusing, suggests that we can develop a relationship with these inner parts of ourselves, and, befriending them, diffuse their impact on our lives. (For more information on Focusing, a bodily oriented process of self-awareness developed by Eugene Gendlin, see the Resources section at the back of this book.)

When we struggle against these parts, pushing them aside, we strengthen them. In not wanting to give them voice or expression, we keep them even more alive within us, rather than less.

If children tug at your sleeve, you might take a moment or two to let them know that you hear them. You may be busy right now, but at another time, you promise, you will give them your full attention. In the same way, if I am wanting to engage in my tantric lovemaking with Richard, but something is bothering me, tugging at me, I can take a moment to acknowledge it. Although I may do this silently, and I often do, it is even more powerful to invite Richard to help me.

The following exercise, called All of Me, helps you stay engaged with your beloved, even while acknowledging whatever part might be pulling you away. When you gently turn toward this part, giving it your brief, yet compassionate attention, it may no longer feel forced to scream or hide. You might find that it willingly releases its hold on you, allowing your fragmented energy to be enfolded back into your essential being.

Within each of us is a sense of singular wholeness, an "all of me," that is infinitely more than the sum of our parts. This core, our essential being, is itself linked to a universal field of energy that resonates in the vibration of all life. I like to think of this as our divine self, or Self, with a captial S. Cornell calls it Self-in-Presence. When we reside in that place in us, we experience an all-inclusive beingness. Rather than identifying as a smaller "part" of ourselves, we're open to a larger, more expanded Self.

In this exercise you are simply saying hello to whatever part of you has shown up, affirming that the part exists, recognizing it as carrying one or more strands of your own precious life energy. You will be asking your partner to help you hold that part of you in your shared heart-space. Doing so will create an intimacy of presence that nourishes your erotic relationship and brings you into loving wholeness with your beloved. For example, I might notice there's something edgy in me, something that doesn't feel relaxed. Rather than entering into a discussion about it, which might not be an appropriate use of our time at the moment, I simply acknowledge it, label it, and ask Richard to help me hold that part of me in our heart-space.

This formal, yet simple, ceremony, opens up an even larger space for the emergence of love and passion. The short, simple phrases create a safe way to help me momentarily turn toward any part of myself with softness. Almost always, when that part of me is acknowledged in this way, my feeling of closeness with Richard develops and deepens. There is no need to know what is causing the edginess, only that, as Cornell writes, "It is so, now."

RICHARD SAYS *Diana notices and is more sensitive to her inner life than I am. I'm not usually interested in discussing emotions and feelings. This practice makes it easy for her to express herself in a way that doesn't overload my short attention span. And I experience a deepening of our connection.*

How to Do "All of Me"

If you first practice this exercise when you feel comfortably and happily connected, it will be easier to remember to do it when something comes up that is separating you from your beloved. Decide together how long you will do the practice. Even a few minutes can be transformational.

❖ Face each other, sitting or lying down. Breathe, and say, "I am here" to each other. Establish a loving heart-space.

❖ Maintain eye connection.

❖ Partner A: Take a moment to notice something you are aware of. It could be an emotion or a body sensation, whether pleasurable or not. It could be a sound you hear or a scent you notice or something you see in the environment. Find one thing. Report it to your partner. Reveal that a part of you is noticing, feeling, or sensing something.

Say to your partner:

"I'm noticing a part of me that feels (wants, doesn't want, hears, smells, sees ...)"

OR "There's a part of me that feels (wants, doesn't want, notices ... etc.)"

OR "I'm sensing something in me that feels ..."

Some examples:

"I'm noticing a part of me that is annoyed by the loud car horns outside."

"There's a part of me that feels silly doing this practice."

"A part of me is aware of the sweet smell of your perfume."

"I'm aware of part of me thinking about work."

"I'm noticing a part of me that is really angry right now."

❀ After stating that you are noticing a part of you, ask your partner:

"Will you help hold *all of me*, including that part of me, here in our heart-space?"

❀ Partner B replies: "Yes, I will help hold all of you, including that part of you, here in our heart-space."

❀ Partner A: "Thank you."

❀ Reverse roles and practice this back and forth for five or ten minutes or for however long you have decided upon. Then use this same format whenever appropriate in your daily lives together.

Note: In a more advanced version of this practice, the partner is asked to repeat back or paraphrase the description of the other partner's experience.

Examples:

"Yes, I will help hold *all of you* here in our heart-space, including that part of you that is feeling so angry right now."

"Yes, I will help hold *all of you* in our heart-space, including that part of you thinking of work right now."

❖   ❖   ❖

In this book I have presented to you a number of ways, both physical and verbal, to intimately connect with your partner. I hope you have found them useful, valuable, and meaningful.

Intimacy Brightens the World

I believe that intimate, tantric loving brings more light to the world and helps make love more available to everyone. That's how important intimacy is. If you are in a relationship, your loving matters.

In the spring of 1982, I wrote my first essay on intimacy. I was on an airplane, leaving my life in northern California to spend a year with my ailing father in Albany, New York. Although I no longer have that essay, I remember the passionate feelings that writing about intimacy aroused in me.

Whenever you are present, you become "transparent" to some extent to the light, the pure consciousness that emanates from…Source.
ECKHART TOLLE, author of *The Power of Now*

I had experienced intimacy on the Aikido mat. Practicing Aikido techniques with a partner, I had shared the stark intimacy of physical presence without a social façade. Although the sharing was not sexual, there was an inherent knowing of one another that took place. With our bodies, we moved into each other's energy field and discovered the power of union.

I had experienced intimacy as a practitioner and teacher of massage at Esalen Institute in Big Sur. Professional massage is not a sexual event. Yet touching someone, guiding that person with my hands into an incredibly relaxed state of body and mind, provides a sacred entry into personal and transpersonal dimensions of intimacy.

> *From every human being there rises a light that reaches straight to heaven. And when two souls that are destined to be together find each other, their streams of light flow together and a single brighter light goes forth from their united being.*
>
> THE BAAL SHEM TOV, rabbi, founder of Hasidic Judaism, 18th Century

I had experienced intimacy during meditation, both the intimacy of eyes-open practice with my sitting partners and the inner intimacy of overwhelmingly pure love. It was beyond sexual, beyond anything I had ever previously known. To enter quietly into the depths of my own soul and share that journey consciously with others in real time creates an unimaginable intimacy.

I play the flute, and I experienced intimacy with other musicians as we jammed and improvised our way through sound and rhythm.

I had experienced intimacy with close friends, revealing to each other the joys and pains of our ever-changing emotional landscapes.

And, yes, I had experienced sexual intimacy with other lovers.

But in 1982, when I wrote an essay about intimacy, I had not yet discovered the sacred, loving intimacy that tantric sex has made possible in my marriage. At our wedding in 1985, Richard and I promised each other that we would learn together "what it means to *love* another person for a whole lifetime." Although sexual intimacy is only one aspect of the love we share, it is indeed a significant aspect. Tantra Tai Chi has provided us, and the couples who attend our Intimacy Retreats, with a reliable pattern for **S**ynchronized **E**nergy e**X**change. Now you, too, have access to this teaching, an opportunity to share a rewarding spiritual path with your partner.

> *Far away in the heavenly abode of the great god Indra, there is a net hung in such a manner that it stretches out indefinitely in all directions. A single glittering jewel hangs at the net's every node....*
>
> THE AVATAMSAKA SUTRA, translated by Francis H. Cook

I would like to leave you with one final note. When a couple is happily in love, everyone around them benefits—their children, friends, even strangers on the street. So lovemaking is not only good for you, it is good for those you love. And there is even more. Sometimes when Richard and I are embraced in Peaceful Passion, I seem to transcend to a place outside the planet. I become aware of a grid, a network of intersecting lines that surrounds the whole globe. At each intersection, a couple's loving causes a light to shine. Without such love, the earth would surely dim. I later discovered a Buddhist teaching that describes just such a grid, called the web of Indra, with brilliant jewels positioned at each node, reflecting each other infinitely. In my own vision, each of those jewels is a couple making love.

Sacred lovemaking is therefore not only a delightful and rewarding personal adventure but also a valuable civic responsibility!

Each time you experience sacred, sattvic, tantric sex with your partner, even if it is only for ten minutes, please remember that because of you, the light and love continue to shine more brightly for all of us. Thank you for joining me on this global mission.

Global Loving

APPENDIX

Testimonials from Couples Who Have Studied Tantra Tai Chi

❄   ❄   ❄

"We went into this retreat looking for something to bring us back together the way we were when we first met, but what we received was a connection that surpasses first love."

— *Rusty and Cherie*

"It was our eighth anniversary; we wanted to get away and dedicate a weekend just to us. We had noticed that recently there were times when we felt close, and other times when we didn't feel close. We didn't know what to do about it, other than go have sex or something, which really didn't work to bring us closer. We both knew we wanted this deeper connection, this deeper intimacy."

— *Nancy and David*

"We wish we had learned this when we were first married, twenty-five years ago!"

— *C. and G.*

"I consider myself to be an average American guy—I like to drink beer, watch football, and fish. This workshop was Lisa's idea, and I went along because I love her and knew how important it was to her. I would have rather gone fishing. That was looking forward. Looking back after the experience, I was sorry to see it end. Somewhere between arriving and departing, I did a complete '180.' The setting, coupled with your insightful guidance, leadership, and camaraderie, made this the best vacation I have ever taken. I came away totally rejuvenated. Lisa and I hug and giggle all the time. We act like little kids with a secret. Our passion has been rekindled and we are closer now than we've been in a long time."

— Ben and Lisa

"My beloved and I truly valued our experience. We were at a crucial time in our relationship—almost to the point of going our separate ways. The retreat has given us hope for getting back what we were missing. With the easy-to-use Tantra Tai Chi exercises, we now have tools we can use to build and maintain an intimate relationship."

— L. and R.

"This workshop with its unique combination of Tantra and Tai Chi has had a very powerful impact on our lives. The connection we experienced in our personal relationship has had a lasting effect, and, more importantly, continues to grow as we practice."

— M. and H.

"We feel so much more connected now and believe that we have such a solid foundation on which we can keep building. Chad was very thankful to meet a role model like Richard—we rarely see men be open like that. I also appreciate the modeling of women as 'goddesses.' I can already feel the empowerment of that belief, not only sexually, but in all areas of my life. I am so excited for the next participants, thinking about what a tremendous opportunity they are about to experience."

— Rachel and Chad

"We learned to bring intimacy to us instead of waiting for it to show up. The weekend truly enriched our togetherness more than you know."

—*J. and D.*

"He's glowing. We're both glowing. He's showing up more openly, peaceful, loving, and listening more. Hmmmm…how about that!"

—*B. and M.*

"When we arrived on Friday night, we were filled with frustration and loss of our connection. When we left on Sunday, we could not stop singing and laughing with joy. We were blissfully in touch again with our feelings of love for each other and the universe. The weekend was filled with stimulating ideas to reestablish bonds with each other and with ourselves. Bravo to you and your work!"

—*Maram and Larry*

"I recommend the Intimacy Retreat for all couples wanting to preserve and improve their intimate sexual connection."

—*James M. Fitts, MD, urologist*

"We are an interfaith couple; we have struggled for fifteen years to find a way to share our spirituality together. At the Intimacy Retreat, gazing into each other's eyes, we finally found it."

—*Peter and Maria*

GLOSSARY

Chinese, Japanese, and Indian Words Associated with Tantric Sex

❉   ❉   ❉

Aikido (Japan): A martial art based on energy awareness and harmonious resolution.

amrita (India): Female ejaculate, "sacred nectar." Also, the scent of a saint. Any soft flow that is meditatively inspired.

Ayurveda (India): Ancient medical system emphasizing the balance of energies in body, mind, and consciousness. Uses herbs, aromas, nutrition, massage, lifestyle changes, yoga, cleansing methods, and so forth.

bindi (India): A ceremonial dot placed on the third eye; the crystallization of energy in the center of the head, at the pineal gland. Part of the Tantra Tai Chi™ trilogy.

Buddhism (India): A spiritual life practice based on the teachings of the Buddha, with a focus on awakening, nonattachment, and spiritual community.

chakras (India): "Spinning Wheel." Primary energy centers that correspond to physical and glandular locations in the body, from the base of the spine to the top of the head.

chi (China): Spiritual energy, life force. Also spelled *qi*.

chi kung (China): Energy practice. Also spelled *qigong*.

dakini (India): Female practitioner of Tantra. Said to be able to enlighten a man through her sex.

dantien (China): Primary center of energy storage in the body. There are three: lower, middle, and upper. Translates to "field of elixir." Also spelled *tantien*.

deva (India): Divine being from another realm of existence, who can bestow blessings on others.

feng shui (China): The art of placement of self and objects, used to positively harness universal forces and reduce their negative impact. Translates to "wind and water"; circa 2000 B.C.

gassho (Japan): Greeting, salutation, bow. (See *namasté*.)

guna (India): A particular grouping of qualities, tendencies, or aspects of human nature. (See *rajasic, sattvic*, and *tamasic*.)

guru (India): A spiritual teacher or guide.

hara (Japan): The lower dantien; abdomen. Used as the focus for centering in Aikido. Also as a character trait meaning courageous, gutsy, or principled.

Hinduism (India): A religious tradition rooted on the Indian continent, based on belief of the world as "maya," or illusion, as compared to an ultimate reality.

hui yin (China): Perineum point, between the anus and the sexual organs.

jing (China): The original energy or life force that is stored in the lower dantien. Also refers to male ejaculate, sometimes referred to as "loss of jing."

Kama Sutra (India): Training manual of sexual techniques and rules of love. *Kama* translates as "sensual desire" or "pleasure"; a *sutra* is an "essay." Thought to have been written between the first and sixth centuries. Translated into English in 1883.

ki (Japan): See *chi*.

kundalini (India): Energy resting at the base of the spine, like a coiled snake awaiting the journey upward through the chakras. A kunda is a bowl in which fire burns.

lingam (India): Penis; translates as "wand of light." (Also spelled lingham.)

maithuna (India): Ceremonial sexual intercourse for conscious union with the divine.

mantra (India): Sacred chant.

mudra (India): Sacred gesture or hand position.

namasté (India): Greeting, salutation: "I honor the divinity within you." Generally accompanied by a bow, with the hands held in prayer position. (See *gassho*.)

nirvana (India): A heightened state of awareness that is unattached and transcends normal mental activity; enlightenment.

om (India): The original, primal sound of creation, a mantra. (Also spelled aum.)

prana (India): Breath, spirit, energy.

qi (China): See *chi*.

qigong (China): See *chi kung*.

rajasic (India): The aspect of human nature that is passionate, ambitious, and active. Rajasic sex is amorous, playful. and goal-oriented. (See *tamasic* and *sattvic*.)

Reiki (Japan): Energy healing through hand placement and use of symbols.

samaya (India): A vow or sacred bond, usually between guru and disciple.

Sanskrit (India): The sacred language of ancient India.

sattvic (India): The aspect of human nature that is calm, pure, spiritual, and balanced. Sattvic sex is conscious, energy-based, and meditative. (See *tamasic* and *rajasic*.)

Shakti (India): Primal energy that is sexually released and activated by the female. Creative energy. Also name of a Hindu goddess.

Shiva (India): The stillness of pure consciousness, a space held by the male. Also name of a Hindu god.

T'ai Chi (China): A form of exercise or martial art that is based on the flow and power of inner energy. Also spelled taiji.

tamasic (India): The aspect of human nature that is lethargic, depressed, or out-of-balance. Tamasic sex can be boring or abusive. (See *rajasic* and *sattvic*.)

tantien (China): See *dantien*.

Tantra (India): A spiritual path that embraces sexual energy for conscious awakening.

Tantra Tai Chi™: Movements to enhance the energy of intimacy on all levels—physical, emotional, and spiritual.

tantrika (India): Practitioner of Tantra.

Tao (China): Translates as "The Way" and is held to mean the absolute, ultimate truth; the formless source.

Taoism (China): A spiritual practice of following the Tao.

vajra (India): Literally "thunderbolt"; in Tantra used for the penis.

yab yum (India): Physical and spiritual union of male and female energies. Upright lovemaking position, sitting-on-lap, face-to-face.

yang (China): Half of the created universe; having qualities such as hot, dry, bright, linear, outward moving, or masculine.

yantra (India): Visual aid to meditation.

yin (China): Half of the created universe; having qualities such as cool, moist, dark, relational, inward, or feminine.

yoga (India): Disciplined practice leading to higher consciousness.

yoni (India): Vagina; translates as "sacred valley" or "sacred space."

Resources

❖   ❖   ❖

Workshops

Intimacy Retreats: Richard and Diana Daffner, MA, offer weekend, weeklong, and private couples' retreats, held in romantic resort locations. Intimacy Retreats are an opportunity to personally experience the heart of tantric teachings and to deepen the love connection in your relationship. With humor, knowledge, and sensitivity, the Daffners provide couples with educational tools to transform a relationship into a love affair.

    tantra2@IntimacyRetreats.com
    www.IntimacyRetreats.com
    (877) 282-4244   (941) 349-6804

For a listing of other Tantra workshops offered worldwide, see www.Tantra.com/workshops.

CDs/DVDs

Lessons in Intimacy…The Lover's Touch, CD (Dynamic Resources, 2003). This audio-book will guide you and your beloved into a real experience of tantric love. It is also available as a digital download at www.LessonsinIntimacy.com.

Tantra Tai Chi for Lovers, DVD (Dynamic Resources, 1999). *Tantra Tai Chi for Lovers* provides DVD instruction and demonstration of the Tantra Tai Chi exercises. Information about this product can be found at www.TantraTaiChi.com.

Ancient Secrets of Sexual Ecstasy (Higher Love Video, 2006).

Tantra Products

www.TasteofTantra.com

Sells bindi dots, sensual gifts, and other products to enhance your relationship.

Books

Cupid's Poisoned Arrow: From Habit to Harmony in Sexual Relationships by Marnia Robinson (Random House, 2009).

Everything Tantric Sex Book by Bobbie Dempsey (Adams Media, 2007).

Life's Too Short for Tantric Sex by Kate Taylor (Da Capo Press, 2003).

Making Love: Sexual Love the Divine Way by Barry Long (Barry Long Books, 2006).

Red-Hot Tantra: Erotic Secrets of Red Tantra for Intimate, Soul-to-Soul Sex and Ecstatic, Enlightened Orgasms by David Ramsdale and Cynthia Gentry (Quiver, 2004).

Resurrecting Sex: Solving Sexual Problems and Revolutionizing Your Relationship by David Schnarch (Harper Paperbacks, 2003).

Soul Sex: Tantra for Two by Al Link and Pala Copeland (Career Press, 2008).

Super Marital Sex by Paul Pearsall (Doubleday, 1987).

Tantra: The Art of Conscious Loving by Charles Muir (Mercury House, 1990).

Tantric Sex by Suzie Hayman (Carlton Books, 2008).

Tantric Sex for Women: A Guide for Lesbian, Bi, Hetero and Solo Lovers by Christa Schulte (Hunter House Publishers, 2005).

Tantra for Erotic Empowerment: The Key to Enriching Your Sexual Life by Mark A. Michaels, Patricia Johnson, and Tristan Taormino (Llewellyn Publications, 2008).

The Art of Sexual Ecstasy: The Path of Sacred Sexuality for Western Lovers by Margo Anand (Tarcher, 1990).

The Heart of Tantric Sex: A Unique Guide to Love and Sexual Fulfillment by Diane Richardson (O Books, 2003).

The Lover Within: Opening to Energy in Sexual Practice by Julie Henderson (Barrytown Limited, 1999).

Touch Me There! A Hands-On Guide to Your Orgasmic Hot Spots by Yvonne K. Fulbright (Hunter House Publishers, 2007).

Urban Tantra: Sacred Sex for the Twenty-first Century by Barbara Carrellas (Celestial Arts, 2007).

Sexual Massage

Female Ejaculation and the G-Spot: Not Your Mother's Orgasm Book! by Deborah Sundahl (Hunter House, 2003).

Tantric Massage: The Erotic Touch of Love by Kenneth Ray Stubbs (Rider & Company, 2004).

The Tao of Sexual Massage: A Step-by-Step Guide to Exciting, Enduring, Loving Pleasure by Stephen Russell. (Revised edition. Fireside, 2007).

T'ai Chi

Embrace Tiger, Return to Mountain: The Essence of Taiji by Chung-Liang Al Huang (Celestial Arts, 1988).

T'ai Chi Chih! Joy Thru Movement by Justin F. Stone (Good Karma Publishing, 1996).

Focusing and Other Communication Trainings

Focusing by Eugene Gendlin (Bantam Books, 1982). www.Focusing.org.

Nonviolent Communication: A Language of Life by Marshall Rosenberg (Puddledancer Press, 2003).

The Power of Focusing: A Practical Guide to Emotional Self-Healing by Ann Weiser Cornell (New Harbinger Publications, 1996). www.FocusingResources.com.

The Five Love Languages: How to Express Heartfelt Commitment to Your Mate by Gary Chapman (Northfield Publishing, 1995).

Feng Shui

www.JamiLin.com provides custom complimentary best-direction and bagua maps.

T'ai Chi/T'ai Chi Chih/Aikido Training

www.Ai-Ki-Do.org
www.TaiChiChih.org
www.LivingTao.org

Tantra Tai Chi

For information about a teaching certification program in Tantra Tai Chi, see www.TantraTaiChi.com.

About the Author

❊ ❊ ❊

DIANA DAFFNER, MA, is a member of the Coalition for Marriage, Family and Couples Education (CMFCE) and the Association of Sexuality Educators, Counselors and Therapists (AASECT). In 2002 she received a certificate in Sexology and Human Relations from the Midwest Institute of Sexology. She holds a BA in psychology from Cornell University and an MA in counseling from Webster University, and has taught meditation, massage, and movement arts for over thirty-five years. Drawn toward the experiential qualities of Eastern philosophies, Diana is a teacher of T'ai Chi Chih® and Reiki and has spent time in a Zen monastary. Having earned a black belt in Aikido, she is featured in the book *Women in Aikido*.

With her husband, Richard Daffner, she developed Tantra Tai Chi™ as an intimacy exercise and has conducted romantic Intimacy Retreats for couples for over ten years. The Daffners produced a CD, *Lessons in Intimacy...The Lover's Touch*, which provides listeners with a guided introduction to sacred sexuality, and a DVD of their Tantra Tai Chi program. They can be heard on radio shows coast-to-coast and have spoken at universities, international healing forums, and annual conferences, such as Smart Marriages and the Society for the Scientific Study of Sexuality (SSSS).

Diana's writings have appeared in numerous print and web publications, and she serves as an expert in sacred sexuality for personal growth websites. She and Richard currently live in Siesta Key, Florida, where, in addition to workshops, she provides marital coaching and performs wedding ceremonies. She is known locally for her heart-inspired flute playing.

If you wish to contact the author, e-mail her at diana@DianaDaffner.com.

Index

❊ ❊ ❊